G000252274

The Ev
f(
BIGFOOT
AND OTHER MAN-BEASTS

An assessment of what we currently know about the
North American Bigfoot and other apparently related
creatures.

The Evidence
for
BIGFOOT
AND OTHER MAN-BEASTS

JANET AND COLIN BORD

Series Editor: Hilary Evans

THE AQUARIAN PRESS
Wellingborough, Northamptonshire

First published 1984

British Library Cataloguing in Publication Data

Bord, Janet
    The evidence for bigfoot and other man-beasts --
(The evidence series)
1. Sasquatch
I. Title   II. Bord, Colin
001.9'44   QL89.2.S2

ISBN 0-85030-363-X

*The Aquarian Press is part of the
Thorsons Publishing Group*

Printed and bound in Great Britain by
Whitstable Litho Ltd., Whitstable, Kent

CONTENTS

'THE EVIDENCE' Series is prepared by The Aquarian Press in collaboration with ASSAP (Association for the Scientific Study of Anomalous Phenomena). Each book in the series will give a comprehensive, impartial and up-to-date assessment of the evidence currently available for a particular phenomenon.

Each book is written by a recognized authority on the subject who is in a position to give both a comprehensive presentation of the facts and to analyze them in the light of his own experience and first-hand research.

●

ASSAP (Association for the Scientific Study of Anomalous Phenomena) was founded in 1981 to bring together people working in different fields of anomaly research. It does not compete with other societies or organizations, but serves as a link organization enabling members of existing groups to share views and information and benefit from pooled resources. ASSAP issues its own publications, has its own research archives, library and other facilities, and holds periodic public conferences and training events in various parts of the country: ASSAP co-operates with local groups or, where none exists, may form one of its own.

ASSAP members include people from all walks of life who share a belief that it is the scientific approach which is most likely to solve these enigmas: they are neither uncritical 'believers' on the one hand, nor blinkered sceptics on the other, but are ready to go where the evidence leads them. If you sympathize with this attitude and would like to participate actively in our exciting pursuit of truth, you may consider joining us. Write for fuller details to the Editor, Evidence Series, Aquarian Press, Denington Estate, Wellingborough NN8 2RQ.

ILLUSTRATIONS

Cover: Frame from a cine film of Bigfoot taken by Roger Patterson, 20 October 1967, at Bluff Creek, northern California, USA. Photo: Patterson/Gimlin, © 1968 Dahinden, via Fortean Picture Library.

ACKNOWLEDGEMENTS

We wish to record our appreciation of the invaluable work being performed by investigators and researchers in all corners of the world. They have provided the evidence from which this book has been compiled. Some other examinations of the evidence published in book form are listed in the Bibliography, while up-to-date information on new developments in man-beast research can be found in several magazines which publish such data:

Bigfoot Co-op, 14602 Montevideo Drive, Whittier, CA 90605, USA.
Fortean Times, BM-Fortean Times, London WC1N 3XX, UK.
INFO Journal, PO Box 367, Arlington, VA 22210, USA.
The ISC Newsletter, International Society of Cryptozoology, PO Box 43070, Tucson, AZ 85733, USA.
Pursuit, SITU (The Society for the Investigation of the Unexplained), PO Box 265, Little Silver, NJ 07739, USA.
UFONS (UFO Newsclipping Service), Route 1 – Box 220, Plumerville, AR 72127, USA (has a section devoted to Forteana News).

The photographs are reproduced by kind permission of René Dahinden/Fortean Picture Library; except for numbers 10, 11, and 12, which come from Dr Zhou Guoxing/Fortean Picture Library.

Any readers possessing firsthand information on man-beasts are requested to send it to the authors c/o the publishers.

ONE:
BIGFOOT IN NORTH AMERICA

I was flabbergasted! At a distance of perhaps 8 to 10 yards [7-9 metres], I could clearly see that their bodies were covered in hair that was short and black as a Labrador Retriever's. One was walking a few steps ahead of the other and appeared to be clutching something to its left upper torso. The one behind was an inch or two taller than the first; I would guess it to be five foot seven or eight inches [1.7 metres] in height as measured against the windscreen of the car. This creature half turned towards me, and for a moment I could see the flash of a white eyeball and the obvious bulge of its male genitalia. I noticed too its hands – thick, elongated and strong looking.

Their heads were low-set on broad shoulders and their skulls were flat and sloped back from heavy brow ridges to a sort of conical topknot – almost like the beginning sagittal crest of a young gorilla. Their bodies were gangly rather than heavy or muscular, and perhaps because of this, I had the distinct impression that they were young or youthful members of their species. I cannot remember detecting facial features, nor can I say whether this part of their anatomy was dark skin or dark hair . . .

To the right of my car there was a sharp vertical six foot [1.8 metre] high embankment that on the other side dropped away quite steeply. The smaller creature paused at the foot of this incline, then flexing its legs in a standing broad jump posture, sprung easily to the top. It then dropped over the other side from my view. The larger creature quickly followed, ascending the bank in two steps, as effortlessly as a man might go up stairs. It was an extraordinary display of locomotion; impossible, I am convinced, for any human to duplicate.[1]

The speaker was 54-year-old Donald Hepworth, a Chief Inspector with the Ontario Humane Society and formerly with Canadian Military Intelligence and the London Metropolitan Police Force. He was describing his encounter on 7 April 1980 with two specimens of a species whose very existence is hotly disputed. But if Donald Hepworth did not see Bigfoot, what did he see? Although it was growing dark as he drove along US Highway 95 through Payette National Forest in Idaho, the creatures he saw were clearly illuminated by his car headlights, and only 25-30 feet (7.5-9 metres) away. A man who has handled apes and bears as part of his job is unlikely suddenly to be unable to recognize them, and at the same time to describe what he sees in such detail – detail which in several respects echoes the reports of other Bigfoot witnesses.

Donald Hepworth is certainly not alone in claiming to have seen this unbelievable animal (or human?), thought by many (few of whom are within the scientific community) to be living in considerable numbers in the wilder parts of the North American continent. How reliable the sighting reports and other evidence are, we shall try to assess in this book. But if the sceptics are right and there is no such creature as Bigfoot, then it is a fact that thousands of Americans and Canadians are either prone to hallucinations, or compulsive liars, or unable to recognize bears, deer and vagrants.

A proportion of the witnesses undoubtedly do fall into one of these categories, but it is hard to believe that all of them do. We collected together over 1,000 sighting reports in our *Bigfoot Casebook*, and it has been estimated that for each sighting reported, ten go unreported for various reasons, possibly the most frequent being the witnesses' reluctance to expose themselves to ridicule. In addition to the sighting reports there are many reported findings of Bigfoot footprints, an aspect of the evidence which we shall explore in Chapter 4.

Early reports

Bigfoot is not just a phenomenon of the 1970s and 1980s. The earliest report we have dates back to 1818, when 'a gentleman of unquestionable veracity' saw a hairy, man-like creature in the woods near Ellisburgh, New York State.[2] Despite a thorough search of the area by hundreds of pursuers, nothing more was seen or heard of this 'wild man of the woods' (as such creatures were known in the nineteenth century) – and this is a familiar feature of twentieth-century Bigfoot reports: a sighting followed by the creature's apparent total disappearance. Is this explained by an ability to move quickly through difficult terrain, or is there a more esoteric explanation?

Since compiling *Bigfoot Casebook* more early reports have come to light. The earliest of these is for January 1869, when a wild man is said to have attacked a carriage near Gallipolis, Ohio. The creature pulled to the ground a man who was travelling with his daughter, and in the ensuing struggle the father was saved from death by his daughter, who threw a rock at the wild man. This hit it on the head, whereupon it gave up the struggle and retreated to the woods. [3] A wild man seen each autumn near Morgantown in Pennsylvania was,

according to the statements of those who have seen him, nearly seven feet [2 metres] high, and weighs over two hundred and fifty pounds [114 kilograms]; he walks generally on all fours, is almost covered with hair, gives unearthly yells and makes all kinds of gestures. His hands and feet are double the size of an ordinary man's, and he presents altogether a horrible appearance. He approaches the cabins of the settlers in the mountains, carries off their pigs and sheep, and with a demonic laugh, disappears in the dense forests. The brave spirits of the neighborhood go gunning for him, but whenever they come in sight the monster gives a yell and a jump, and before the hunters have time to pull trigger he is gone.[4]

Although this press report dates back over 100 years, to 1874, it contains many features that are confirmed by today's reports: height, weight, hairiness, vocalizations, large hands and feet, a habit of approaching rural settlements, stealing livestock, an ability to disappear fast when danger threatens. Even the regular annual appearance is not unprecedented, since some researchers believe that Bigfeet follow the same travelling routes from year to year, possibly following food supplies; and they have also been reported as sometimes moving on all fours, as did the Morgantown wild man.

Section of a photograph of an unidentified creature lying dead in the snow. It was shot by trappers at Lillooet, British Columbia, Canada, early in the twentieth century.

That Bigfoot reports have changed little during 100 years is shown by this press report from August 1982, describing a close sighting at Ellington, Connecticut, by two farmhands.

David Buckley and John Fuller told police they were about to check on the cows at Valley Farms on Route 83 shortly before midnight Monday when they came upon the creature.

'We almost had a heart attack – we were about 2 feet [0.6 metres] away from it,' Buckley said this morning.

Buckley described 'it' as about 6 feet [1.8 metres] tall, weighing 300 pounds [136 kilograms], with immense muscles, long, dark-brown hair over its entire body, arms that hung down to its knees, ominous dark eyes and a 'good set' of dangerous-looking teeth, according to Buckley. And a nose that resembled a human's more than a monkey's snout.

'We walked around the back and we saw it on a feed bunk, sitting right on the edge of it, like a person,' he said. 'It was watching the cows, and it had its hand down in the silage and was either playing in it or eating it.'

The creature turned and got up quickly, saw the two employees, and in what Buckley said might have been a gesture of friendliness, walked towards Fuller slowly. But neither man was interested in making friends. Buckley said Fuller, the farm's night manager, screamed and neglected to ask the visitor its name.

The mysterious cow-watcher then veered towards Buckley, its arms outstretched. Buckley screamed. 'We had the impression he wanted to have us for dinner,' he said.

After Buckley screamed, the creature turned, ran slowly around the corner of the feeding bins and 'vanished into nowhere,' Buckley said.

Buckley and Fuller, still in shock, ran the other way and called the police. 'I've never seen a human with a build like that,' Buckley told the police. 'Not even the muscle builders.'

State police at the Troop C barracks in Stafford thought the two men were stoned. 'At first they didn't believe us,' said Buckley. 'Then, ah, I guess they started believing what we had to say. They went up with us to look for him.'

While Buckley and Fuller searched the area with a trooper, another officer drove up the road by some cornfields along which Buckley believes the strange visitor may have fled. Nothing was found.[5]

Unable to come up with any satisfactory (to them) explanation for the two men's report, the police later stated that the culprit may have been someone in a gorilla suit. This is an often-used solution to the mystery, but fails to take into account the average American's attachment to firearms, and the likelihood that he will ask no questions when confronted by a tall, hairy monster but will shoot wildly at it, as has often happened. Any human willing to don a gorilla suit in these circumstances must enjoy risking his life.

Bigfoot in Indian lore

Although it was not until 1958 that a real interest in Bigfoot developed nationally (when Jerry Crew discovered 16-inch [40 centimetres] long and 8-inch [20 centimetres] wide barefoot tracks around his tractor on a remote logging road in northern California), there were plenty of reported sightings published in local newspapers (and presumably many also went unreported) during the previous decades, and all these pre-1958 reports show that the Bigfoot phenomenon has been widespread throughout the United States at least since the beginning of the nineteenth century and probably even earlier than that. American Indian lore contains references to various forest monsters, and some researchers have suggested that these are descriptions of Bigfoot. They include the Wendigo/Windigo/Witiko, a cannibalistic monster reported by the Algonkian Indians, the Stoneclad, who are stone-covered giants of Cherokee lore, and many others. But there is little positive evidence to show that the majority of these monsters are descriptions of Bigfoot. As Raymond D. Fogelson, a professor of anthropology, comments: 'I think these related myths and monstrous beings concern universal human problems. They involve rationalizing the inevitable existence of evil in this world, particularly in the form of fear, suffering, disease and death.'[6] However, since most anthropologists and ethnologists do not believe that Bigfoot exists, they would be unlikely to support a Bigfoot interpretation for *any* of the Indian lore, some of which does seem to be describing the creature we today call Bigfoot.

Indeed if Bigfoot does exist, it is highly likely that the Indians, being very familiar with the forests, would have come across the creature on many occasions. Some records seem to confirm this, for example the records kept by Spanish priests in the 1770s which stated that an area along the Santa Ana River east of Chino in southern California was the domain of Towis or Takwis, a giant hairy cannibal. This 'devil' was said to stink of rotten meat, and to wander about at night, both Bigfoot traits. The Gabrielino Indians considered this 'devil' to be a real creature, not a ghost or spirit.[7]

Also very real was the Bigfoot described by Wintu Indian medicine woman Flora Jones to researcher Tom Muzila in 1978 when he visited her home in the Lake Shasta area of California. She told him that the Bigfeet lived in caves, and that her people would sometimes find very large human-like bones there. The Wintu Indians considered the Bigfeet to be a giant Indian tribe and traded tobacco with them, being the only northern Californian tribe able to get along with them. She said that Bigfoot ages slowly, and also has 'a very slow birth rate'; there are now only a few left in northern California. Flora Jones, commented Tom Muzila, was 'very withdrawn from modern society' and liked to think over the things she heard round the campfire in her younger days.[8] If Bigfoot researchers had in the past talked to Indians still in touch with the Indian way of life, before it was contaminated by the twentieth century, they would most likely have tapped a good source of Bigfoot lore.

At one time it was thought that Bigfoot lived only in the west and north-western area of the North American continent – the states of California, Oregon, Washington, and over the Canadian border into British Columbia. Even today there are some researchers who will only take seriously reports from those areas. But there are too many from other parts of the continent for them all to be ignored. Bigfoot has been sighted in most American states, from Florida in the far south-east (42 reports of the 1000 in our *Bigfoot Casebook*) to Alaska in the far northwest (10 reports). Research has shown that reports from

René Dahinden hunts for Bigfoot during 1974 in the Stave River area 40 miles (64km) north-east of Vancouver, British Columbia, Canada. This is typical Bigfoot country in North America.

those states away from the north-west have a tendency to contain unexpected features, such as Bigfoot's ability to remain unaffected by gunfire (the next case is an example of this), and other aspects which might suggest that perhaps some Bigfeet are not entirely physical. (We shall discuss this important aspect of Bigfoot research later, in Chapter 5.) But apart from points of detail, the majority of Bigfoot reports follow the same pattern: a Bigfoot encounters a human being by design (through curiosity, as when it visits rural settlements) or by accident (as when a hunter in the forest unexpectedly sees a Bigfoot). Usually, but perhaps not unexpectedly, this encounter is swiftly concluded as the human witness escapes in terror! The following three cases give some idea of the kind of reports being made in the 1980s, across North America.

The Fulton case: Kentucky, 1980

It was a warm October night in 1980 when Charles Fulton and his family were visited by a 7-foot (2.1 metres) tall, white-haired Bigfoot at their rural home in Mason County, Kentucky. As they were sitting watching television, they heard someone trying the back door knob. When Fulton went to investigate, he found a strange creature standing on the porch holding a rooster. His mother-in-law also saw it close to, and commented: 'I never saw anything like it in my life. It just looked like a big white fuzzy thing standing on the porch. I never saw its face; it was above the 7-foot-high [2.1 metres] door.' It jumped off the porch, and as it stood in the yard Fulton shot at it twice with his .22 pistol. 'I know I didn't miss, but the creature didn't even flinch or make any sound when I shot. It just stood there for a moment. It could have killed me if it wanted to.'

Another strange feature noticed by Fulton was that when the creature left, although it walked like a human being, it seemed to move in slow motion. Bigfoot usually can retreat very fast when startled, but if this one really was immune to gunfire it presumably had no need to move fast! Fulton was certain the creature was not a bear, nor a gorilla, nor a man in costume. Newspaper coverage of the events brought Fulton unwanted publicity (he received calls from reporters in thirty-eight states) and he was ridiculed by many people who did not want to believe his story, a fate suffered by most witnesses who publicize their Bigfoot encounters. But eighteen months after the' events, Fulton was steadfast: 'I don't care whether people believe it or not, I know what I saw. I quit drinking 15 years ago, and I don't pop pills.'[9]

New Jersey, 1981

Bigfoot is not seen frequently in Kentucky (16 reports out of 1000 in *Bigfoot Casebook*), and another eastern state with few reports is New Jersey (15 reports). But two fisherman got close enough to a Bigfoot in May 1981 to be quite positive that it was nothing familiar to them. Said one: 'I'll go to my grave knowing it wasn't a bear or anyone in a suit. I don't expect to ever see anything like that again.' The two were returning home at night from a fishing trip in the 35,000-acre Newark Watershed when a large creature strode across the dirt road ahead of them. They saw it clearly in the station wagon headlights, and decided to follow it down a dirt path. They were as close as 5 feet (1.5 metres) to it when they got stuck in mud. They described the creature as 'semi-human', about 6½ feet (2 metres) tall, weighing just over 300 pounds (256 kilograms) and covered with reddish-brown hair. Its face was flat, and its ears were like a man's. It walked with a slight hunch, arms swinging and fists clenched, 'like a cross-country skier would move', and seemed oblivious to the presence of the vehicle and its occupants.[10]

The Freeman case: Washington State, 1982

The most widely reported sighting of 1982 took place in traditional Bigfoot country, the forests of Washington State. This close but brief encounter was enhanced by the finding of top quality footprints. The witness was Paul Freeman, a 39-year-old US Forest Service patrolman working in the Umatilla National Forest in the Walla Walla area. At 11.30 a.m. on 10 June he was alone in the forest.

It was a beautiful sunny morning and I was about half a mile outside the perimeter of the watershed. I got out of my truck because I'd seen some elk on a ridge and I wanted to see if they had any young. I walked up an old logging spur which had windfalls over it so I couldn't drive. Suddenly I saw something step off a bank about 10 feet [3 metres] high and down on to the road. I saw him about the same time as he saw me. He looked like all the pictures I've seen of prehistoric man. He was real hairy – reddish-brown hair. It was so thick you couldn't see through it on his shoulders, arms and legs. But on his face and chest it was thin enough to see his skin, the colour of brown leather.
     I was about 65 yards [59 metres] away from him and I just stood there looking at him and he looked at me. I could hear him breathing real heavy as though he'd been running and I could see the muscles in his stomach moving. But that was the only noise he made. I was scared and I started backing away a few feet. He made the hair stand up on his neck and shoulders just like a dog does when it tries to frighten someone . . . When he saw I wasn't coming any further he turned and walked up the road.

Freeman is 6 feet 5 inches (1.9 metres) tall and weighs 265 pounds (120 kilograms), but the Bigfoot was about 2 feet (0.6 metres) taller, and very heavy. Freeman was convinced that he was not looking at a bear, with which he was very familiar, or a man in a gorilla suit – he could see the muscles moving in its legs, arms and shoulders. 'I've been working in the wilderness for years and . . . never seen anything like it.'
     Shortly after telephoning them from a forest service

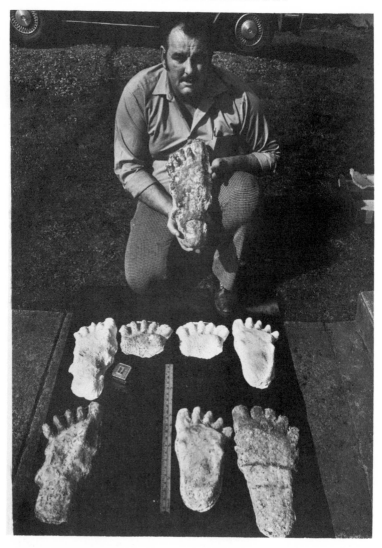

Paul Freeman, who saw a Bigfoot and its footprints on 10 June 1982 in Umatilla National Forest, near Walla Walla, Washington State.

cabin, Freeman was joined by colleagues, and together they photographed and took casts of the footprints left by the creature. They found twenty-one tracks, each 14 inches (35 centimetres) long by 7 inches (17 centimetres) wide, and 6-8 feet (1.8-2.4 metres) apart. A week or so later, more tracks were found close by. Some were an inch (2.5 centimetres) deep in moist ground, and there were apparently two creatures, each estimated to weigh about 600 pounds (272 kilograms).

Dr Grover Krantz, a professor of anthropology at Washington State University who has been studying Bigfoot tracks for years, was very impressed by the prints: 'I think these may be the best set of prints of a Sasquatch* ever obtained.' His statement was based on the discovery of skin patterns known as dermal ridges. These fine lines would be exceedingly difficult to fake, and they show that the feet which made the tracks belong to a higher primate, but not an ape or a human. 'They come from a higher primate that doesn't exist so we have an interesting problem here,' Dr Krantz commented at a press conference held at the University of British Columbia in October 1982 by the International Society of Cryptozoology.[11] However, despite the apparently high quality evidence, there is not unanimous acceptance of the validity of the Freeman case by all Bigfoot researchers, and at the time of writing investigations are continuing.

Typical witness descriptions

Paul Freeman's sighting could be taken as a pattern for Bigfoot sightings in general. He saw a tall, hairy, man-like creature walking upright on big feet. It left deep footprints showing that it weighed much more than any man; it was seen only briefly; and it seemed at home in the forest. Although many reports in general agree with Freeman's, we find both variations and similarities among

---

*An alternative name for Bigfoot, of American Indian origin.

witness descriptions of features they especially noticed.

The great height and bulk of Bigfoot is a particular feature remarked on by many witnesses. Freeman's Bigfoot was around 8 feet (2.4 metres) tall, and 6-8 feet (1.8-2.4 metres) seems to be the height most often reported. Occasionally an extra-tall Bigfoot is reported, 10, 12, or even 15 feet (3, 3.6, or 4.5 metres) tall. Some of these witnesses may have unconsciously exaggerated the height, their judgement being affected by their feelings of fear and amazement. But sometimes the witnesses of extra-tall Bigfeet have been able to assess the creatures' heights fairly precisely. In June 1965 two prospectors near Pitt Lake in British Columbia, Canada, found 24-inch-long (60 centimetres) tracks in the snow and followed them until they noticed a creature on the hillside not far away. It seemed to be watching them, so they sat down to watch it. By using their knowledge of the trees' growth rate, they were able to roughly judge the creature's height. One man said 10-12 feet (3-3.6 metres), the other said 12-14 feet (3.6-4.2 metres). In Alberta, also in Canada, five men working on the Big Horn Dam construction site in August 1969 were similarly able to judge the height of a mystery visitor from a comparison with the trees behind it. It stood watching the men for about half an hour, and afterwards some of the men went over to the place. Those who stayed behind were amazed to see that the men were only about a third as tall as the creature that had stood watching them. By a conservative estimate, therefore, the creature was at least 12 feet (3.6 metres) tall, possibly 15 feet (4.5 metres) or even more.[12]

Very occasionally, witnesses describe small creatures. In July 1955 there were several sightings of 'a hairy little grey man without clothes' near Edison, Georgia. Tant King, a farmhand, was the first to see it when he was mowing alfalfa. The creature was about 3½ feet (1 metre) tall and walked upright from the woods and along the fence-line. Although frightened, King watched for twenty-five minutes until the creature wandered back into the woods. Fresh tracks presumed to be the creature's were found: 'about the size of a hand with four claws turned out sideways'; and over the next few days two women, mother and daughter, saw the little man on separate occasions.[13] A more recent report of a similar nature came from Bruce in South Dakota, where three thirteen-year-olds claimed in September 1979 to have seen a monkey-like creature 2½-3 feet (0.7-0.9 metres) tall on several occasions. Brownish, with big ears and no tail, the creature ran very fast on two legs, and one boy got to within 20 feet (6 metres) of it.[14] It is interesting to note that some of the earliest Bigfoot reports, dating from the 1830s, described small creatures or 'wild children', hair-covered and around 4 feet (1.2 metres) tall.[15]

Bigfoot's hairiness is another feature which all witnesses notice. The hair colour is usually recalled, and this can be black or white, or many shades in between – red, blackish-red, reddish-brown, light brown, dark brown, dark grey, bluish-grey, whitish grey, silvery white, tan, fawn, beige.. These are just some of the colours named by the witnesses, the darker shades being most often reported. Sometimes an unusual combination of colours is mentioned. The female Bigfoot seen at close quarters by William Roe on Mica Mountain, British Columbia, in October 1955 had dark brown, silver-tipped hair,[16] while a 7-foot (2.1 metres) Bigfoot encountered by two hunters near Bend, Oregon, in October 1977 was black with silver fur at the shoulders.[17] Very occasionally, Bigfeet with a fair ruff or mane have been seen. The Traverspine 'gorilla' (Labrador, 1913) had a ruff of white across the top of its head; a Bigfoot nicknamed Yellow Top (Cobalt, Ontario, 1923 and 1946) had a light mane; and one seen near Lancaster, Pennsylvania, in 1973 was grey with a white mane.

The length of hair also varies, usually appearing to be short, but sometimes noticeably long. The head hair is often longer than the body hair. A man who saw a Bigfoot near Beausejour in Manitoba said that it had long hair flowing from the back of its head down on to its shoulders.[18] The hair texture is sometimes rough or matted, sometimes smooth or neat. A man living near Granite Falls in Washington State saw a Bigfoot in August 1980 to which both hair descriptions aplied. From the waist down the hair (strawberry coloured with some grey in it) was smooth and shiny, but from the waist up it was matted and tangled, long and tight like ringlets. He felt that this showed that the creature moved from place to place along the creek, walking waist-deep in the water.[19]

Few people have actually touched a Bigfoot, but thirteen-year-old Tina Barone may have done so. The Barone family live on a farm in Brockway Township, Michigan, and in November 1981 some unknown creature was scaring the family and farm animals with its night-time high-pitched screams, prowling around and tearing down fences. One evening Tina and Roxanne (12) went out to the barn to check on their horses which had been disturbed. As she reached for the light switch Tina felt some fur. 'At first I thought it was a goat or something, so I took my glove off and I touched it again,' she said. But the beast that she saw glaring down at her with bright-red eyes was no gloat. It was 2 feet (0.6 metres) taller than the girls, and 'its fur was about one inch [2.5 centimetres] thick and all matted and dirty.' Tina's mother doubted that the animal was a Bigfoot as investigators suggested, and when she learned that a tame bear had escaped from a nearby resident two years before, she identified that as their mystery visitor. But Michigan Department of Natural Resources wildlife biologists were doubtful, saying that a bear would have been observed. 'Bears are very visible. They aren't nocturnal, and they have no natural enemies – so they don't try to hide. It isn't very likely one could be here without seeing it.'[20]

Witnesses often do not see Bigfoot closely enough to be able to describe its head and face in detail. Also fear and surprise tend to inhibit the witness from carefully memorizing each individual feature. But from a consensus opinion it would seem that Bigfoot has a flat face and a large, flat nose, a heavy brow ridge, and a short neck or even no neck at all. William Roe, whose 1955 sighting we mentioned earlier, was able to sit and watch a female Bigfoot eating from a distance of 20 feet (6 metres). He studied her face closely, and noted her flexible lips, white and even teeth, broad and flat nose, lips and chin protruding further than the nose, ears shaped like a human's, small and black eyes like a bear's. Although the face was hair-covered, it was bare around the mouth, nose and ears, and the hair was short. The neck was 'unhuman, thicker and shorter than any man's I have ever seen'. Another careful description of a Bigfoot head and face was given by Mrs Louise Baxter, who was watched by a Bigfoot as she checked her car tyres near North Bonneville, Washington State, in August 1970. It was still daylight, and though terrified, Mrs Baxter noted that

The creature was coconut brown and shaggy and dirty looking. It had one huge fist up to its mouth. The mouth was partly open and I saw a row of large square white teeth. The head was big and seemed to set right onto the shoulders. The ears were not visible due to the long hair about the head. It seemed the hair was about two inches [5 centimetres] long on its head. It had a jutted chin and receding forehead. The nose and upper lip were less hairy and the nose was wide with big nostrils.[21]

It is interesting to compare these descriptions with the Russian researcher Dmitri Bayanov's drawing of the head of the female Bigfoot seen and filmed by Roger Patterson at Bluff Creek, California, in October 1967. Bayanov made his drawing (see page 100) by studying frames of the film in minute detail. We can see clearly the heavy brow ridge and broad, flat nose, protruding lips and short neck. There is also another prominent feature: a pointed head.

This feature occurs occasionally in witness descriptions. Two men driving near Edgewood, Iowa, on 13 January 1980 saw a Bigfoot in their car headlights. Seven feet (2.1 metres) tall, it had a large chest, very long arms, and a 'sort of pointed crown of hair or bone' on top of its head, with long hair reaching down to its shoulders.[22] Dr John Napier commented in his book *Bigfoot* on the 'cone-shaped top to the skull' of the Bigfoot filmed by Roger Patterson. This bony crest is a non-human feature, but occurs in adult male gorillas and orang-utans, its function being 'to give supplementary attachment areas for heavy jaw muscles necessitated by massive jaws and teeth'. He adds that it is rarely seen in females, yet the creature filmed by Patterson was definitely a female, with heavy breasts.

If many of the facial details go unnoticed by most witnesses, the eyes quite often excite comment. 'Red' and 'glowing' are words often used, in fact red is the colour most often reported, followed by a number of reports of green eyes, and a few each of yellow, amber, white, and black, with variations on these colours like greenish-yellow and blue-green. Mrs Louise Baxter, whose 1970 encounter was quoted earlier, especially noticed the creature's eyes. They 'were the most outstanding as they were amber colour and seemed to glow like an animal's eyes at night when car lights catch them.' Also in Washington State, the creature seen near Granite Falls in 1980, mentioned earlier, also had glowing amber eyes, very deepset and wide apart. Glowing red eyes, often huge – 'as big as lightbulbs' (Marshall, Michigan, 1956) – seem to be reported most frequently in those areas away from the 'traditional' Bigfoot terrain in the north-west, and are associated with the weirder reports that we shall consider later. But red eyes do occur in reports from the north-west, such as the Yakima, Washington, sighting on 19 September 1966 made by Ken Pettijohn. During a violent storm, Pettijohn skidded and stalled his car. In the headlights' glow he saw a greyish-white, 7-foot (2.1 metres) creature, with flat nose, thin lips, and red eyes, almost fluorescent, shining in the car lights. When asked for more information on the eyes, Pettijohn was unable to add any details, commenting: 'I wasn't concentrating on staring him in the eye.'[23] Dr John Napier explains the phenomenon of 'eye-shine' or retinal reflection in his book *Bigfoot*,[24] and comments that the eyes of nocturnal animals show green, those of diurnal animals show red, pale-pink or white.

Moving downwards, past the short or non-existent neck, the creature's body is usually described as heavy and broad-shouldered, and the creature itself stands erect, or slightly stooping. Male genitals are rarely noted, but females have noticeable breasts, such as the Bigfoot seen by Charles Jackson and his young son at their small farm near Oroville, California, on 12 July 1969. They were standing watching a bonfire they had built, when a noise behind them made them turn, to see a hairy creature 8 feet (2.4 metres) tall standing by an old building about 15 feet (4.5 metres) away. 'It had a quizzical look, sort of puzzled, at first, as if it was wondering what we were doing. Later, I thought it must have been near man before. It wasn't alarmed by us.' But Mr Jackson and his son were alarmed, and ran indoors. The dogs too made for cover, most untypically. Mr Jackson gave a full account of this sighting to investigator René Dahinden, who visited him a few days afterwards, and Dahinden was most impressed by his story.

It was like both an ape and a human. It had longer legs than a man, It was upright and when it walked away later it swung its arms like a human. The chest area and the face were almost bare and the face was like that of a negro, the skin almost black. Its palms were paler, almost yellowish. At the shoulder it was between three and four feet [0.9-1.2 metres] wide and there were huge bulging muscles, and no neck. Its arms were massive, very muscular, and it had long fingers. It had great flat breasts that hung down to the navel area. The hair on its head was like that of a woman who hadn't washed it for months. It was light grey with what seemed to be caked mud on it. Its feet were about fourteen to fifteen inches [35-38 centimetres] long and were very flat and very wide.[25]

Mr Jackson noticed massive, muscular arms. Witnesses sometimes describe these as being rather long, as did the two hunters near Pitt Lake, British Columbia, in June 1965, mentioned earlier. Their Bigfoot had long arms dangling down to below the knees. Bigfoot hands are usually large, but like human hands. Claws are rarely mentioned, and then only in the weirder reports away from the north-west. The legs are human-like, as is the creature's walk, though it often has a long stride. Dr Dmitri D. Donskoy, a Russian expert in biomechanics, analysed the movement of the Bigfoot filmed by Roger Patterson and stated that although the walk was human-like, it was more like the way humans walk when cross-country skiing, with excessive knee bending. Its walk showed that the creature was heavy, with strong and well-relaxed muscles used more effectively than man uses his. At one point in the film the sole of the creature's foot is visible, and it can be seen that the foot has no arch, unlike the human foot. Dr Donskoy comments that 'Lack of an arch may be caused by the great weight of the creature.'[26] Bigfeet have left many footprints of varying quality for study by researchers (see Chapter 4), but there are few witness descriptions of Bigfoot's foot, for obvious reasons. So the evidence of the Patterson film is especially valuable, and what can be seen on the film does tie in with what has been learned through the study of the clearest footprints.

Having described the 'typical' Bigfoot, it is perhaps worth noting that there are of course exceptions to the majority descriptions, some of them rather strange but most of the

Charles Jackson and son at Oroville, California, showing where they saw a Bigfoot on 12 August 1969.

peculiarities being described by more than one witness, their sightings well separated in time and space. For example, there are a few reports of Bigfeet with tails. One seen widely by farmers around Albany, Kentucky, in the autumn of 1973 had a long black bushy tail,[27] and the word 'bushy' was also used to describe the tail of a Bigfoot seen at Mamquam, British Columbia, in June 1969.[28] Both these creatures left tracks showing only three toes.

Douglas Trapp holds plaster casts he made of Bigfoot tracks 14½ inches long and 5 inches wide (37 x 12cm), which he found beside the Stillaguamish River near Verlot, Washington, on 5 September 1980.

We also have a few reports of Bigfeet going down on all fours, though they were also seen to walk upright. The reports we have on record come from Labrador (1913),

Ohio (1964 and 1968), and Indiana (1962 and 1972). Other peculiarities include pointed ears, a greenish glow, horns, no arms, head bigger than body, fangs, and three legs, but some of these descriptions are likely to be a result of misperception caused by fright.

Too often reported to be caused by imagination, fright, or coincidence, is the presence of a foul smell. We have on file many vivid phrases which show what a strong impression the smell made on the witnesses, almost as strong an impression as the sight of the Bigfoot itself! A few sample descriptions from recent reports follow.

'odor was indescribable – a really sick smell – like something dead' (Malad, Idaho, August 1980)

'like unwashed armpits' (Blackfoot Reservoir, Idaho, July 1980)

'like an uncovered septic tank' (Northwest River Park, Virginia, June 1981)

'sewer odor stronger than the smell of the hogs' (Vici, Oklahoma, early 1982)

'it stunk like a half-rotten bear hide' (Mount Shasta, California, September 1976)

'rank and sickening . . . something like a decaying meat and vegetable combination' (Sharpsville, Indiana, June/July 1971)

'like a dog that hasn't been bathed in a year and suddenly gets rained on' (Tavernier, Florida, July 1977)

However, by no means all Bigfoot witnesses report a bad smell. John Green, a Canadian researcher who has the largest collection of Bigfoot material, says that only 5.6 per cent of reports contain any reference to a smell.[29] If there had been one, as overwhelming as those noted above, the witnesses would surely not have forgotten to mention it. Several explanations have been put forward: that the smell is a result of the creature rummaging in rubbish or walking through sewers; that Bigfoot rolls on rotting carcases; that the smell is glandular and controlled by the Bigfoot and is intended as a defence mechanism, to keep people at bay. However, Ivan T. Sanderson, a zoologist who made a close study of man-beasts, was not surprised by the many reports of strong-smelling creatures. In his book *Abominable Snowmen: Legend Come to Life* he gave several examples of smells he had experienced, including the nauseating stench given off by the 'nice little Pigmies' of the Congo Ituri Forests in Africa. The primates are the greatest stinkers, according to Sanderson,[30] so this may be another clue to Bigfoot's identity.

TWO: BIGFOOT IN THE HIMALAYAS AND USSR

Although this book concentrates on the North American Bigfoot, as being the most reported and publicized specimen of hairy man-beasts, such creatures are also seen in many other parts of the world. In fact, all the continents except Europe have living traditions of man-beasts and it is probable, judging by the folklore of many European countries, that there were once man-beasts in Europe too. That continent is now too densely populated to allow such creatures to live in the seclusion they prefer, and the remaining mountainous or sparsely populated areas are apparently an unfavourable habitat, possibly because of lack of food sources.

In all the other continents, there is still enough uninhabited terrain with suitable flora and fauna to support groups of man-beasts, and from time to time sighting reports reach the media from remote corners of the world. One reason why the North American Bigfoot has become so well known is that the witnesses are very media-orientated, and many will not hesitate to announce their sighting to the world through the newspapers. In some other countries where man-beasts are seen, the witnesses probably rarely see newspapers and it would not occur to them to report their sightings. Most of the reports have been obtained by travellers visiting the remote areas and asking if anyone has seen man-beasts. So we cannot base an assessment of the number of surviving man-beasts on the number of published reports, and the North American Bigfoot population may well be exceeded by those of better hidden, less reported man-beasts living deep within the Asian, African, Australian and South American continents.

If we call these creatures 'man-beasts' or by their local names, this distinguishes them from the North American Bigfoot, for there is no certainty that the same creature is being reported all over the world. Some may be forms of men, others may be giant apes. Each man-beast has been given a name, often many names, in its own country, as Bigfoot/Sasquatch has in North America, and we will begin our lightning tour of the world's wilderness areas with the Himalaya mountains, the home of the best-known man-beast – the Yeti or Abominable Snowman.*

The Yeti

Although this is the best-known man-beast, it may also be one of the least seen. Most of the evidence for the existence of the Yeti takes the form of footprints in the snow. An early report, though not the earliest, from a reliable source, is found in *Among the Himalayas* by Major L. A. Waddell, who journeyed from Darjeeling to north-east Sikkim in 1889 and in his book reported his own sighting of footprints:

Some large footprints in the snow led across our track and away up to the higher peaks. These were alleged to be the trail of the hairy wild men who are believed to live amongst the eternal snows, along with the mythical white lions whose roar is reputed to be heard during storms. The belief in these creatures is universal among Tibetans. None, however, of the many Tibetans I have interrogated on this subject could ever give me an authentic case.[1]

*The latter is a translation of 'metoh kangmi', the name used by native porters.

Despite Major Waddell's lack of success with the native population of the Himalayas, later explorers found plenty of people who claimed to have actually seen the creature, as we shall relate.

In the hundred years since the Major saw what may have been a Yeti's footprints, many other Himalayan explorers have made similar reports and, as with the North American Bigfoot, footprint sightings outnumber visual sightings of the creature itself. The decade 1970-80 was particularly fruitful for footprint sightings. In December 1972 Edward W. Cronin, Jr, an American zoologist working as chief scientist of the Arun Valley Wildlife Expedition, and Dr Howard Emery discovered a series of tracks in the snow outside their tent 12,000 feet (3.600 metres) up on Kongmaa Laa Mountain in eastern Nepal. The 8½ x 4¾ inch (21 x 12 centimetres) tracks, clearly showing a fat big toe, four smaller toes and a wide, rounded heel, suggested a creature weighing 165 pounds (75 kilograms) and walking on two legs, and Cronin could reach no other conclusion than that a Yeti had paid them a nocturnal visit. The tracks were very similar to the one photographed by Eric Shipton twenty-one years earlier and many miles distant.[2] Two years later, members of a Polish climbing expedition found footprints 14 inches (35 centimetres) long at the base of Mount Everest. Again the creature was apparently heavy, and bipedal, since the men saw the tracks continuing for over a mile in single file. Team leader Andrew Zawada commented: 'In my 29 years of climbing experience in Europe and Asia, I have seen footprints of bears but what I saw at the base of Mt. Everest makes me believe in the unbelievable.'[3]

Mountaineers Peter Boardman and Joe Tasker were not so outspoken when commenting on their own brush with a mystery creature early in 1977, yet they could not deny the strangeness of the event. They were camping at 17,000 feet (5,100 metres) on Changabang in the Himalayas, surrounded by ice and snow and in a temperature of 18 below zero. During the night they were woken by the crash of their cooking equipment being knocked over, and heard scuffling and growling noises. They wisely decided to postpone investigation until daylight. Then they found that only one item was missing – a carton containing 36 chocolate bars. The thief had left 12-inch (30 centimetres) footprints leading to and from the tent. Joe Tasker commented: 'No living thing could exist at that height without food and in sub-zero temperatures – yet something did. A Yeti? Who knows?' Yeti or not, it seems to have known what it was looking for. The chocolate bars were wrapped in plastic and packed in rucksacks with the rest of the food. The year before, Joe Tasker and Dick Renshaw, then climbing on nearby Dunagiri, lost chocolate bars in similar circumstances.[4]

Lord Hunt, leader of the 1953 Everest expedition, has seen strange footprints on several occasions, the most recent being in 1978 during his trek across Nepal to commemorate the 1953 expedition. Lord and Lady Hunt found a line of fresh 14-inch-long (35.5 centimetres) prints, obviously made by a heavy creature breaking through hard snow on which a person of normal weight made no impression. They also saw other sets of tracks, and Lady Hunt suspected the creature was curious about their camp and looking for food.[5] These are only some of the footprint discoveries during the 1970s. The recurring feature of tracks found at mountain campsites strongly suggests curiosity about humans and their activities, and even a realization that the presence of humans means the possibility of easy food. Such behaviour is also typical of the North American Bigfoot.

Although actual sightings are not numerous, there have been a few good reports. Perhaps the earliest reliable one comes from Lt. Col. C. K. Howard-Bury and his mountaineering companions, who in 1921 were attempting to climb the North Face of Mount Everest. Through binoculars they watched a group of dark spots moving across the snow at about 23,000 feet (6,900 metres), and when they reached the place they found enormous footprints. A closer sighting was made in 1925 by N. A. Tombazi, who was a Fellow of the Royal Geographical Society on a photographic expedition in the Himalayas. At about 15,000 feet (4,500 metres), near the Zemu glacier, his porters alerted him to a human-like figure 200-300 yards (180-270 metres) away. The creature was walking upright and pulling at dwarf rhododendron bushes. It looked dark against the snow and seemed to be without clothes. It was soon lost to sight among thick bushes. Later Tombazi was able to pass the place where he had seen the creature, and found manlike footprints 6-7 inches (15-17 centimetres) long.[6]

As well as sometimes having their own sightings of tracks or creatures, some European travellers have been able to talk to reliable native witnesses. Charles Stonor, a scientist with a team that visited the Himalayas in 1954 specifically to hunt for the Yeti, collected several fairly recent reports. Sherpa Pasang Nyima said he had seen a Yeti only three months before. It was the size of a small man, and had long hair on its head, body and thighs, but less hair on its face and chest. It walked upright and seemed to be grubbing for roots. When it realized it was being watched, it cried out and ran off into the forest, still on two legs. Another small Yeti was watched from the safety of a hut in 1949 by Mingma, a Pangboche villager. It moved with long strides and was slightly stooped. Mingma could see its face and noticed a squashed-in nose, a high, pointed head with a crest of hair, a hairless face except for brown hair on the sides of the cheeks, and large teeth. These he saw when the creature noticed him through the crack in the wall, and growled and showed its teeth.[7]

In November 1949 a large group of Sherpas including Sen Tensing saw a Yeti from about 80 feet (24 metres). The men were gathered at the Thyangboche monastery for a religious festival. The monastery stands at a height of about 13,000 feet (3,900 metres), and the Yeti suddenly came out of the forest. This grey-haired, man-sized Yeti, showing an unusual lack of concern for its safety, wandered around in the snow, scratching itself, grunting, and playing with the snow, until driven away by the noise of the monks' gongs, horns and trumpets.[8] There are rumours that Yetis have been captured by Nepalese tribesmen, but they died in captivity and the corpses were not kept.[9]

The only solid remains, apart from scalps, which are highly controversial, seem to have been excreta found by the 1954 expedition. Analysis revealed a diet of mice, birds, vegetable matter, and earth. Natives said that the Yetis ate small rodents, large insects, and clayey earth, the last perhaps for its mineral content. They were also suspected of taking young yaks and deer, and in fact they probably are totally omnivorous, eating anything they can obtain – with a special penchant for chocolate bars![10]

If sceptical Westerners are loth to take seriously reports made by mere inhabitants of the Yetis' terrain, they might give more credence to a report made by another famous British mountaineer, Don Whillans, after his 1970 expedition to Mount Annapurna. While searching for a campsite one evening, he heard a sound like bird cries and the Sherpa identified it as a Yeti. Whillans briefly saw a black shape on the ridge in the distance. Next day he found mansize tracks 18 inches (45 centimetres) deep in the soft snow. That same evening, while camping, he felt that the creature was still around, and stuck his head out of the tent. By moonlight, and with the aid of binoculars, he watched a black, apelike shape pulling at snow-covered tree branches. After twenty minutes, perhaps realizing that it was being watched, it disappeared at speed.[11]

From descriptions collected over the years, researchers have been able to build up a picture of the Yeti's physical appearance. Professor René von Nebesky-Wojkowitz, who spent three years in Tibet and Sikkim, commented in his book *Where the Gods are Mountains*[12] that information gathered from different areas of the Himalayas was not contradictory. The creature was said to be 7-7½ feet (2.1-2.25 metres) tall, covered with dark brown hair, having long arms, an oval, pointed head, an apelike face, and with less hair on the head and face. The professor's description of the Yeti's behaviour and habitat contain important clues to the identification of the creature. He said that it lives in 'the impenetrable thickets of the highest tracts of Himalayan forest', where it spends the daytime asleep. It moves around at night, travelling through the forest on all fours, or swinging from tree to tree. It emerges on to the snowfield in search of a certain 'saline moss'. Ivan Sanderson thought that this 'saline moss' is probably a lichen rich in vitamins,[13] and Bernard Heuvelmans laid emphasis on the Yeti's behaviour, saying that it is only bipedal when moving across snow, which is not its normal territory.[14] But before drawing any conclusions from this, we must comment on the variations in size of the creature and its footprints as reported by witnesses.

It seems, according to a Tibetan lama, that there are two or even three kinds of Yeti. The *nyalmo* are carnivorous giants 13-16 feet (3.9-4.8 metres) tall, living in the snow above 13,000 feet (3,900 metres); the *rimi* are 7-9 feet (2.1-2.7 metres) tall, living at between 10,000 and 13,000 feet (3,000-3,900 metres), and eating plants as well as animals; and the *rackshi bompo* are man-sized, possibly the same as the *yeh-teh* or *mi-teh* described by the Sherpas. These leave the small footprints so often seen, and may be the young of the *rimi*, rather than a separate species. The *rimi* leave larger prints, and are the dark figures sometimes seen, as for example by Don Whillans, and probably the same creature as described by Professor von Nebesky-Wojkowitz. The *nyalmo* is the most elusive, and may be only a myth.[15]

Over the years many explanations for the Yeti reports have been mooted, usually involving known animals. The footprints have been explained as an illusion caused by the sun, its heat melting and distorting animal tracks and making them appear larger; but in most cases this is unlikely: the tracks are too clear, or obviously fresh, or have penetrated too deep into the snow. Also, animal tracks are closer together than genuine Yeti tracks, and animal tracks which melt and enlarge will get closer together and sometimes even merge. Of all the known animal candidates, the bear is the most likely, since there are bears in the Himalayas, and they do sometimes walk upright. But not always, and bear tracks are usually recognizable as such, though caution is needed because of certain similarities between bear and human footprints which in melting snow can cause the two to be confused.[16] Those witnesses who have actually seen Yetis do not believe them to be bears. The langur monkey, with two species in the Himalayas, has also been put forward as a candidate, but langurs do not exceed 4½ feet (1.3 metres) on their hind legs, and there are also several good reasons why the Yeti footprints could not be Langur prints. This creature would also leave marks of its tail in the snow.[17] The suggestion that Hindu hermits, living high up in the Himalayas, are responsible for Yeti stories is also unlikely; their physical appearance does not match the reports, and their feet, even though naked, would not leave large enough tracks.

Despite numerous foreign expeditions and the accumulated knowledge and experience of the native peoples, the Himalayas largely remain a mystery zone where unknown species could easily be quietly and secretly existing as they have done for millenia. The terrain is not all inhospitable, and that it still can hide secrets is shown by the fact that early in 1982 an Indian army expedition trekking across the lower Himalayas reported that they had come across a group of naked cave dwellers who did not know about fire and ate raw meat. They were frightened by the appearance of their visitors, and seemed to have had no contact with the outside world.[18]

Until a Yeti is killed or captured, there can be no certainty as to the identity of this most mysterious Himalayan denizen, but Professor Heuvelmans believes it to be a large bipedal anthropoid ape, possibly related to Gigantopithecus, a giant primate of which a few remains have been found in China.[19] Desmond Doig, a journalist who has spent thirty years in the Himalayas and has investigated Yeti reports, believes it is a species of the great orangutan which is known to have once lived in the jungles of the Himalayan foothills. He says that people who have seen a Yeti, when shown pictures of various animals including bears and orangutans, invariably select the latter as closely resembling what they saw.[20] Dr George Schaller, who has studied gorillas in Africa, examined casts of the fresh footprints found by Edward W. Cronin, Jr, on Kongmaa Laa and said that they 'demonstrate a close resemblance to those made by the mountain gorilla'.[21] In view of the variations in Yeti reports, it seems possible that more than one type of creature is responsible, some of them animals, some of them unknown human-like creatures.[22]

The USSR, Mongolia and China: the Almas

People often speak of the Yeti or Abominable Snowman as if it were an isolated phenomenon confined to the Himalayas. In fact, the vast mountain range of which the Himalayas are just one area extends east into China and west into the USSR, and in both these regions man-beasts are also regularly reported.

The area of Asia which is the richest in man-beast lore stretches from southern Mongolia in the east (the Gobi desert and Altai mountains), and extends west for several thousand miles through Dzungaria and the Tien Shan mountains (northern Sinkiang, which is itself a part of

China to the north of Tibet), further west into the southern USSR through the Pamir mountains, Kazakhstan, Tadzhikistan and Uzbekistan, as far as the Caucasus mountains between the Caspian and Black Seas. Sightings have also been reported from the northern wasteland of Siberia.

In these areas reports of footprints in the snow do not predominate, as they do in the Himalayas, and most of the data consists of reported sightings of a man-beast, or Almas. This word is the name for man-beasts commonly used in Mongolia, and we will also use it for man-beasts through the USSR, rather than introduce confusion by changing names as we move from region to region. 'Almas' is also one of the simplest when compared with some of the fifty-plus names used in the USSR and Mongolia, like Hü Har Göröös (Black Man-Beast), Snezhnyy Chelovek (Snow Man), Gul'biyavan (Wild Man), Zhapayy Kishi (Wild Man). Other widely used names are Chuchunaa (north-east Siberia), Dev (Pamir Mountains), and Kaptar (Caucasus Mountains).[23]

In this small book it is impossible to do more than include a representative selection of the most interesting sighting reports from the USSR, Mongolia and China, and we will start this brief survey in the Mongolian Gobi Desert, where in 1934 two men travelling by camel noticed a strange two-legged creature covered in short wool watching them. It ran away, followed by the men on their fast-moving camels. The men waved rawhide lassoos, and the creature, on seeing these, cried in such a piercing voice that the camels refused to move and the creature escaped.[24]

On another occasion, a member of a camel caravan travelling through the desert disappeared when he went to collect the camels after resting. The three men who went to look for him found traces of a struggle outside a cave – they saw marks of shoes and of bare feet. They dared not enter the cave, but on their return journey some time later they went back to the place and lay in wait. When a hairy man-beast emerged from the cave they shot and killed it, then rescued their comrade from his captivity. He would never reveal what had happened to him, but remained 'wild and listless' until his death two months later.[25]

These tales were collected by Professor Rinchen of the University of Ulan Bator in Mongolia, who collected information on the Almas in the Gobi Desert and surrounding areas from 1927 until his death in 1978. Professor Rinchen was a scientist, but he was ridiculed in the scientific community. The same fate was suffered by Dr V. A. Khakhlov, a professor of comparative animal anatomy, who in 1913 submitted a report to the Russian Imperial Academy of Sciences on the subject of man-beasts in eastern Asia. These men, and various educated witnesses, were recommended to forget what they had seen and heard about, but fortunately their reports have survived.

Most of Dr Khakhlov's material came from Dzungaria, which is to the south-west of Mongolia, and his witnesses described closer contact with the man-beasts than usually occurs. This is also a feature of reports from regions of the USSR, such as the Caucasus. One witness told Khakhlov that he had helped to capture an Almas by using lassoos, but the creature was allowed to go free when the local inhabitants insisted to the visiting herdsmen who had caught it that the Almas were well known, and not dangerous to man. The captive was a short male, covered with hair 'like a young camel', with long arms, a stooping posture, narrow chest, sloping forehead, massive and chinless lower jaw, small nose with large nostrils, large ears pointed back like a fox's. He also had a strange protuberance at the back of his neck. He moved with bent knees, and his toes were widely separated.

Even more interesting was Dr Khakhlov's report of a female Almas held captive near the River Manas. She, too, was eventually released, but Dr Khakhlov's informant was able to observe her for several months and to describe her appearance, which was very similar to the male just described, and her behaviour. She was usually quiet, but showed her teeth and screeched when approached. She slept like a camel – 'by squatting on the ground on its knees and elbows, resting the forehead on the ground, and resting the wrists on the back of the head'. She would eat only raw meat, some vegetables and grain, though later she also ate bread. She would also catch and eat passing insects. She drank water by lapping, or by dipping her arm and hand and licking the water off.[26]

Scientists in the USSR studying the man-beast mystery today (with more freedom than was allowed to their predecessors) have publicized their work and as a result have received more recent reports from the areas studied by Dr Khakhlov. An old friend and colleague of his living in Kazakhstan passed on some fresh reports, including one from teacher Anatoly Pechersky, who when hiking with two teenage pupils in July 1972 through the Kirghiz mountains was followed by an old male Almas, possibly asthmatic. He tried to steal food from their tent at night and his hairy arm was seen by flashlight as he stuck it through the flap. On one occasion he approached their fire at night and stood only 12 or 13 feet (3.6-3.9 metres) away, but the teacher panicked and went to the tent for his gun. They saw nothing more of the Almas.[27]

Reports of wild men and man-beasts have been current in these areas for centuries, and not just as a part of folklore. A manuscript dating back to the early fifteenth century describes the Tien Shan mountain range, which lies on the USSR/China border in the general area from which the above twentieth-century reports have come.

In the mountains themselves live wild people, who have nothing in common with other human beings. A pelt covers the entire body of these creatures. Only the hands and face are free of hair. They run around in the hills like animals and eat foliage and grass and whatever else they can find. The lord of the territory made Egidi [a Tartar chief, journeying to Siberia] a present of a couple of forest people, a man and a woman.[28]

The Pamir mountain range lies farther south, a westerly extension of the Himalayas and at the point where the USSR, Afghanistan, Pakistan and China meet. Several noteworthy reports have originated there, including a killing in 1925. The story was told by Major-General Mikhail Stephanovich Topilski, who was in command of troops chasing a band of White Army forces through the mountains. They were cornered in a cave, which was then blocked by an avalanche, and a survivor described a fight with hairy man-like creatures in the cave, one of which was buried under the snow. The soldiers dug out and examined the corpse carefully and concluded that it was neither ape nor man. Being unable to transport the body, the men buried it beneath a pile of stones.[29] A few years later, in 1928, a man-beast was captured at a flour mill in the Sanglakh region. It was kept chained up for a couple of months and fed on raw meat and cakes made of barley flour, but it eventually escaped after breaking its chain.[30] A Russian geologist working in the Pamirs in 1926-38, named B. M. Zdorick, was lucky enough to come across a sleeping man-beast while travelling across a remote mountain plateau in 1934. He said that there were drops of blood and scraps of fur, possibly marmot, on the path, and the ground had been dug up. An 'unknown creature' lay asleep, stretched out on its stomach. He could not see the head and front limbs as they were hidden behind a bush, but he could see the legs and feet, which were bare, black and well shaped. The creature's body was covered with shaggy hair like yak's wool, reddish-brown in colour. Zdorick and his Tadjik guide stood and gazed with amazement at the creature for a moment, then the guide pulled Zdorick's sleeve and indicated that they must run away, which they did, the guide's fear now being felt by Zdorick himself.[31]

More recently, the sightings have been less dramatic. In 1954 a Chinese film director, Pai Hsin, saw two creatures walking ahead of him in the distance. They paid no attention to shouts or gunfire. Pai Hsin also found footprints in the snow on another occasion. In August 1957 distant glimpses of a man-like figure against a background of snow were afforded to hydrologist A. G. Pronin, while he was working on the edge of the Fedchenko glacier. From a distance of 550 yards (500 metres), he could not see much detail, but noted the figure's hunched posture and long arms.[32]

Igor Bourtsev holds a cast of a footprint found in the Gissar Range of the Pamir-Alai Mountains in Tadzhikistan, USSR, on 21 August 1979. The print was 13½ inches (34 cm) long and 6½ inches (16 cm) wide at the toes.

In recent years, regular summer expeditions have been made to the Gissar Mountains, which are in Tadzhikistan in the western Pamirs, by a group of people searching for the Almas. They have had some success, finding footprints, getting fleeting glimpses of their quarry, and collecting sighting reports from local inhabitants. The 1979 expedition led by Igor Tatsl found footprints around their tents. Four tracks showed a stride of 4 feet (120 centimetres), twice the average human stride. A week later they found their best print, 13½ inches (34 centimetres) long and 6½ inches (16 centimetres) wide at the toes, and made a plaster cast of it (see photograph on page 48). They also met a local hunter, Gafar Dzhabirov, who claimed to have seen an Almas in the mid-1960s when he was mowing reeds. Feeling uneasy, he looked round and saw a hairy man sitting on a rock 50 feet (15 metres) away, watching him. Gafar grabbed his gun, closed his eyes, and fired in the creature's direction. When he opened his eyes again five minutes later, the creature had gone.[33]

The 1980 expedition lasted for two months, its most dramatic feature being a claim by eighteen-year-old Nina Grinyova that she came face to face with an Almas nicknamed Gosha during a lone night-time walk by the river. She described the events:

He was standing some 25 metres [80 feet] away, facing me and piercing my very soul with his glance. It was not aggressive, rather well wishing, but piercing. The eyes were big and glowing. They were not bright but glowing. And all his body was sort of glowing. He was dark and at the same time, somewhat silvery. I could see his body was covered with hair but it was not shaggy. Maybe it was wet, anyhow the color had a silvery tint. He was about two metres [6.5 feet] tall. His figure looked very hefty, square and straight from shoulder to hip, with a short neck, the head put forward, the arms hanging down freely in a somewhat forward position too.

When I saw him I was not scared and began slowly to advance

to him. Having gone about five steps, I held out and pressed two or three times a rubber toy in the shape of a bird, which made a squeaking sound and was given to me by Tatsl in order to attract Gosha's attention with its sound. But it was this that spoiled our contact. Gosha made a sharp turn and quickly went down the slope to the river and disappeared beyond the steep bank. I noted the softness and grace of his walk, though he moved very fast. It was not a human walk but as of an animal, as of a panther. Despite boulders and other obstacles, he moved quickly, softly and even gracefully. He must have a perfect sense of balance and to him a steep and uneven slope is like a paved road for us.[34]

The group also recorded several sightings by local people, including one in 1975 by a teacher of the Tadzhik language and literature, Loik Yunusov, and his son.

The two of us went to mow grass on a mountain slope and had to spend the night in a ravine. About three o'clock my son woke me up and said someone was approaching us. I then heard someone coming down the slope and later saw two dark figures looking like people but very tall. As they were coming closer they made sounds, imitating now the cackling of a partridge, now the barking of a dog, now the whining of a jackal. When they were bypassing us, some thirty metres [100 feet] away, they must have noticed us and, mumbling angrily, started to advance on us. I fired a shot over their heads from a small-calibre rifle and shouted loudly to drive them away. They ran away down the ravine, but we could not sleep any longer.[35]

One hundred and sixty people joined the 1981 expedition, which lasted for two months from mid-July to mid-September, with additional visits earlier and later in the year. There were no major discoveries or encounters, but several distant sightings were made. Large stones were thrown into one group's campfire at night; and a clear four-toed footprint 19.5 inches (49 centimetres) long was found.[36]

The Caucasus Mountains lie 1,500 miles (2,400 kilometres) further west, and are the source of many good Almas reports. This habitat is isolated from the interlinked mountainous areas just described and forms the last remaining stronghold of the Almas closest to Europe. Like the Gissar Mountains, the Caucasus are the focus of present-day attention by researchers. Dr Marie-Jean Kofman has been studying the subject of man-beasts since 1955, and has lived in the Caucasus on and off since 1959. During her first twenty years she interviewed nearly 4,000 people and in this way she has gathered a formidable collection of data on the Almas. Probably the most amazing report from the Caucasus describes the capture of an Almas in 1941. This creature was examined by Lt.-Col. V. S. Karapetyan, a member of the Medical Service of the Soviet Army, whose report follows:

From October to December of 1941 our infantry battalion was stationed some thirty kilometres [18 miles] from the town of Buinaksk [Daghestan]. One day the representatives of the local authorities asked me to examine a man caught in the surrounding mountains and brought to the district centre. My medical advice was needed to establish whether or not this curious creature was a disguised spy.

I entered a shed with two members of the local authorities. When I asked why I had to examine the man in a cold shed and not in a warm room, I was told that the prisoner could not be kept in a warm room. He had sweated in the house so profusely that they had had to keep him in the shed.

I can still see the creature as it stood before me, a male, naked and bare-footed. And it was doubtlessly a man, because its entire shape was human. The chest, back and shoulders, however, were covered with shaggy hair of a dark brown colour. This fur of his was much like that of a bear, and 2 to 3 centimetres [1 inch] long. The fur was thinner and softer below the chest. His wrists were crude and sparsely covered with hair. The palms of his hands and soles of his feet were free of hair.

But the hair on his head reached to his shoulders partly covering his forehead. The hair on his head, moreover, felt very rough to the hand. He had no beard or moustache, though his face was completely covered with a light growth of hair. The hair around his mouth was also short and sparse.

The man stood absolutely straight with his arms hanging, and his height was above the average – about 180 cm [6 feet]. He stood before me like a giant, his mighty chest thrust forward. His fingers were thick, strong, and exceptionally large. On the whole, he was considerably bigger than any of the local inhabitants.

His eyes told me nothing. They were dull and empty – the eyes of an animal. And he seemed to me like an animal and nothing more.

As I learned, he had accepted no food or drink since he was caught. He had asked for nothing and said nothing. When kept in a warm room he sweated profusely. While I was there, some water and then some food was brought up to his mouth; and someone offered him a hand, but there was no reaction. I gave the verbal conclusion that this was no disguised person, but a wild man of some kind. Then I returned to my unit and never heard of him again.[37]

Lt.-Col. Karapetyan was to learn, many years later, that the prisoner had been shot. Dr Kofman visited the area of the capture in 1959 and eventually managed to track down someone who had taken part in the events.

Only a few years after the 1941 capture, another Almas was trapped, by Mukhamed Tomakov who managed a state farm in Kabardin. This happened in 1946, when Tomakov chased the creature into a mountain cabin. Strangely, it ran on all fours, only standing upright when it stopped running. But this characteristic has occasionally been noted in the North American Bigfoot. Tomakov latched the door and went to get a rope, thinking the creature would be unable to open the door. But he underestimated its intelligence, and when he returned the cabin was empty.[38]

Westerners sceptical of native reports should be frequently reminded of the number of sightings made by outsiders, often men of scientific training and with some standing in the academic world. We have already described several such sightings in this book, and another involved Professor V. K. Leontiev, a professional wildlife conservator who in July 1957 was investigating the Gagan Sanctuary in Daghestan following reports of 'Snowmen'. While trekking alone for a few days at the head of the Jurmut River, he one night heard a strange cry, very loud. 'It wasn't like the yell of an animal – not any wild mammal or bird known to me could make such a sound, and yet it couldn't be a human being either.' The following day he

Left to right: Dmitri Bayanov, Lt.-Col. V.S. Karapetyan, René Dahinden and Marie-Jean Kofman. Taken in the USSR, 1972.

saw a creature crossing a snowfield about 164-196 feet (50-60 metres) away. 'He was walking on his feet, not touching the ground with his hands. His shoulders were unusually wide. His body was covered with long dark hair. He was about 2.2 metres [7 feet] tall.' The professor fired at the creature's feet, hoping to immobilize it, but it was probably too far away and took fright at the noise, running off at high speed.[39]

Despite her long search, Dr Kofman has herself never seen an Almas, only footprints. But from the many eyewitness reports she has gathered, a clear picture of the creature's behaviour has emerged. They live in the mountain caves, in the canyons and forests inaccessible to all but the most skilful and determined climbers. They live off the land, their diet augmented by offerings from the villagers who are well aware of their existence. In the past the Almas used to help the villagers in the fields.[40] In fact it is said that one female, named Zana, was held captive during the last century in the Ochamchir region of Abkhazia. She performed simple domestic tasks such as grinding grain and carrying firewood, and she even had children fathered by a human male (or males). Unfortunately, after each birth she washed the newborn child in the river, and they were unable to survive the cold water. Later the villagers took the babies from her before this could happen, and four survived to grow into almost normal men and women. Zana herself died and was buried at the end of the nineteenth century, but in 1964 Dr Boris Porshnev, another dedicated Russian researcher, was able to visit and talk to two of her grandchildren. He reported that they had dark skin and looked slightly negroid. The grandson had very strong jaw muscles and could pick up a chair, with a man sitting on it, in his teeth. He also had the gift of imitating wild and domestic animals.[41]

Today there are thought to be less than 200 Almas left in the Caucasus. As civilization encroaches on the wild places, their way of life is endangered. They have no natural enemies – except man. But sightings continue, even in areas close to modern civilization. In July 1980 three teenagers mowing grass beside the Nalchik-Pyatigorsk Highway, which is often travelled by foreign tourists, saw a hair-covered creature about the same size as themselves standing watching them. As they watched in amazement, it went through a playful routine as if to entertain them – running to and fro at great speed, jumping, somersaulting. The boys felt it might be inviting them to join it, but they did not have the courage to go nearer, and the creature eventually went off into a nearby hemp field.[42]

The southern mountains are not the only region of the USSR that has proved suitable as a home for the Almas to the present day. Reports emerge now and again from Siberia in the north, where the Chuchunaa are said to be a manlike tribe that follow the reindeer, trapping them for food. In the early years of this century, mineralogist P. L. Dravert reported seeing wild hairy beings along the lower Lena River,[43] while recently USSR's *Technical Journal for Youth* has published a long article detailing a number of sightings during this century and even as far back as 1845, when an Almas was reportedly killed by hunters. Most of the reports come from Yakutia in eastern Siberia, but Almas have also been seen in the region of the Ob River, 3,000 miles (5,000 kilometres) to the west. A former village school teacher told how she had seen the 'Zemlemer', as he was known locally, when she was twenty years old and travelling with her father along the northern Ob and in the Yamal peninsula. Their host promised them a sight of the Zemlemer that night, so:

At midnight, we walked out of the *choom* [tent made of hide or bark]. The moon was already up, big and red. We probably waited about an hour and suddenly the dogs began to bark. Several dozen metres away I spotted a very tall man. Our *chooms* were surrounded by a hedge of rose willows, two metres [7 feet] high. The man's head and shoulders rose above it. He walked fast, with long steps, pushing right through the thickets. His eyes glowed, like lanterns. I had never met such a tall and terrible man. The dogs rushed him, baying. One of them, perhaps brave or encouraged because of our presence, ran right up to him. The man stooped down and having grabbed the dog, he threw it far into one direction. We heard a yelp and saw the dog's body careen through the air. The man quickly walked away and did not turn back to look at us.[44]

In Yakutia, 55-year-old Tatyana Ilinicha Zakharova told how she saw a Chuchunaa in the 1920s while berry picking.

He was also picking berries and stuffing them into his mouth with both hands. When he saw us, he stood up to his full height. He was very tall and lean, more than two metres [7 feet] high, they say. He was dressed in deerskin and barefoot. He had very long arms and on the head, he had shaggy hair. He had a very large face like that of a man but much darker. His forehead was small and protruded over his eyes like the peak of a cap. His chin was large and wide, much larger than that of a man and he was very similar to a human being except he was much taller. After a second, he ran away. He ran very quickly, leaping high after every third step.[45]

Many such events were told to investigators, showing that for a long time there has been a viable population of man-beasts in northern Siberia. But, as elsewhere, the numbers are likely to be declining, and the creatures are withdrawing to the remotest areas.

A glance at the map shows that to the east of Yakutia is the Bering Strait and, not far away, Alaska. It is tempting to wonder whether the Russian man-beast may have travelled across to Alaska in the distant past when the two continents were probably joined by a land-bridge, and established himself in North America. The majority of Bigfoot reports come from the western side of the continent, from Alaska southwards, and it does not seem impossible that such an eastern migration took place at some stage. Ivan Sanderson reminds us that animals such as the moose, elk and brown bear crossed from Siberia to the 'New World', as did Amerinds and Eskimos, so why not man-beasts? Even if there were no land-bridge, a creature used to walking on snow could easily have walked across the solid ice in winter.[46] An alternative route would have been across the more southerly Aleutian Islands. P. L. Dravert was assured by a Yakut tribesman that the Chuchunaa sometimes crossed to the Aleutians, and one was once found lying on the seashore. It lay there all day, no one daring to touch it; then at night it was seen to get up and go away.[47]

In support of the migration theory, there seem to be many similarities between the man-beasts of the Asian and American continents. In 1969 Professor Boris Porshnev published a paper on the Russian man-beast, which included a detailed description of its physical appearance and activities.[48] Among the physical similarities are the variations in hair colour, the short neck, conical head, flat nose, long arms, and its bad smell; while behavioural similarities include an omnivorous diet, night-time activity, and a hostility towards dogs. Some differences are also apparent, especially with regard to the creature's height, which Porshnev gives as usually in the region of 5-6 feet (1.5-1.8 metres), whereas in North America the more usual height is 7-8 feet (2.1-2.4 metres). Porshnev also describes the female's pendulous breasts, which have only infrequently been reported in North America (the Bigfoot seen and filmed by Roger Patterson had large breasts). On the other hand he makes no mention of glowing eyes, which are frequently reported in North America.

Any assessment of the similarities between the Asian

Professor Boris Porshnev.

and American creatures is complicated by the fact that there may be more than one type of man-beast in the USSR. Following his study of the man-beasts of the USSR and Himalayas, Ivan T. Sanderson stated that he had identified five distinct types: '(1) the Mountain Neander-thalers of the West, (2) the little *Almas*; also Neanderthalers, or mere primitives, of the hot deserts, (3) the bestial *Meh-Teh* of the Tibetan upper plateau, (4) the giant *Dzu-Teh (Gigantopithecus), Tok,* or *Sasquatch-type* and (5) the tiny, tropical, forest-dwelling *Teh-lma* of the southern valleys.'[49] Dr Myra Shackley also thinks that some of the Almas may be examples of surviving Neanderthalers, though she does not consider that this identification is appropriate for the North American Bigfoot, or for the creatures recently reported from China.[50] Possible identifications will be discussed in more detail in our final chapter.

THREE: BIGFOOT IN CHINA, AUSTRALIA, SOUTH-EAST ASIA, AFRICA AND SOUTH AMERICA

China's folklore contains many references to wild men, but it seems that not until the 1970s was any real interest shown in the possibility that the tales still emerging from the forests might have some basis in fact. Although there is plenty of isolated terrain in China which might make a suitable habitat for man-beasts, attention is now focused on Hubei Province in central China, as most recent reports have come from there, especially the Shennongjia/Fanxian area. There are thick forests, snow-covered mountains nearly 10,000 feet (3,000 metres) high, and deep valleys with a tropical climate – ideal hideaways for any creature wishing to live in isolation. Several scientific expeditions have visited the area since the mid-1970s, returning with plenty of eye-witness accounts, hairs, faeces, and footprint sightings, but no physical sightings or photographs.

Beginning in March 1977, an Academy of Sciences expedition with 110 members (biologists, zoologists, photographers, and soldiers armed with rifles, tranquillizer guns, tape recorders, cameras and dogs) spent eight months searching for the man-beasts, but they were not successful despite their huge resources, the terrain often being impenetrable. However, the expedition leader, Zhou Guoxing, an anthropologist at the Beijing Museum of Natural History, still believes that an unknown creature is living in the mountains, having spoken to people who have seen it, and having collected evidence in the form of hair and faeces.[1] Late in 1979, scientists engaged in survey work at a height of 8,200 feet (2,460 metres) found a hundred manlike footprints in the snow, varying in size from 8 inches (20 centimetres) to 17 inches (43 centimetres) long. They also found droppings which when analyzed proved to be from a non-human primate eating roots, leaves, fruit and insects.[2]

Shennongjia forestry region in Hubei province, China.

1980 saw two groups of scientists searching for the man-beast, one from the Academy of Sciences based in Hubei Province, the other in Zhejiang Province, where the scientists were originally surveying plant resources until they heard reports of sightings of apemen and as a result extended their expedition. They found footprints, hair samples, droppings, and nests made of branches and lined with grass and leaves. Some were on the ground and some in trees, and their construction indicated a degree of intelligence and strength in the makers. The men also discovered that a biology teacher had preserved the hands and feet of an apelike creature which had been killed in 1957 by a group of women after it had attacked a small girl.[3]

Well over 200 sightings have been reported, some of the accounts vivid enough to convince the scientists that they are not chasing shadows, a belief supported by the tantalizing physical evidence they have found. The earliest sighting report we have seen dates back to 1940, when Wang Zelin, a biology graduate, was working with the Yellow River Irrigation Committee. He and his colleagues saw a 'wild man' that had been shot dead. It was about 7 feet (2 metres) tall, and covered with thick greyish-red

Dr Zhou Guoxing searching for man-beasts in Shennongjia forestry region, China, during 1977.

hair. The face was narrow, with deepset eyes and prominent cheek-bones and lips.[4] Another report of a killing tells how in 1947 Chinese soldiers tracked eight man-beasts through the forest, finally killing and dismembering one of them.[5]

Early in the 1950s Fan Jingquan met a female 'wild man' with a child on two occasions while he was carrying out a geological survey in the Qinling area. He had heard that they were living in the chestnut forest, and persuaded a local man to show him the place. Out of three visits he saw the mother and child twice. His guide had advised a cautious approach, and Fan Jingquan felt that this method should be followed by scientific expeditions. Rather than descending *en masse* into the habitat of an essentially timid creature, they should approach slowly and gradually in teams of two, in order not to alarm their quarry.[6]

There is a jump of twenty years to our next account, given by Zhang Qilin at Xikangli village:

For the past 30 years or more I have gone up to Nine Dragon Mountains, every year around September or October, to guard the maize crop against ape-men. I saw an ape-man about 10 years ago [c. 1970]. It approached from Fengshuyang [where the nests, described earlier, were discovered]. It was about as high as a house door and it was covered in reddish-brown hair with long hair falling around its shoulders and over its face. It walked upright and shook its head as it walked. On another occasion I saw an ape-man lying in a nest in a tree. It was quite relaxed and it clapped its hands when it saw me. Most of the time it just lay there, eating maize, and there was a big pile of cobs on the ground. We know they also like to eat persimmons and wild pears.[7]

The majority of reported sightings took place during the 1970s. This does not necessarily indicate that more sightings were made during that decade, but perhaps it shows that more interest was shown by the outside world, and local witnesses were encouraged to report their encounters. In May 1975 a thirty-year-old stableman named Gan Mingzhi saw a man-beast at close quarters in circumstances that could have been dangerous for him had the creature shown any violent tendencies. When walking near the forest edge,

I heard some noise to my right. I turned, and I was stunned to see a giant standing not far from me. He had hair all over his body and he was over six feet [1.8 metres] tall. I cried out several times, 'help, help'. When I raised my stick to beat him, the wild man grabbed it. He also stepped on my left foot. I was very frightened, but the wild man began to smile, opening his mouth and closing his eyes. Then I felt that the pressure on my foot was somewhat lessened. So I dragged back my foot gradually and stepped sideways. Then I ran away.

It is reported that Gan's fear caused him to be dumb for a couple of weeks, and the local peasants kept away from their work in the fields.[8] But their fear seems unfounded. Throughout the world it is the frightened human witness who acts violently, not the giant man-beast, which could certainly kill a human like swatting a fly, if it wished to. There is much evidence that the man-beasts are harmless and peace-loving, and by approaching with weapons man reveals his feelings of insecurity in the natural world.

Very early in the morning of 14 May 1976, six scientists travelling home by car after attending a meeting in Yunyang, Hubei Province, saw a red-haired creature by the light of their headlamps. It was trying to escape up a cliff, but slipped back and they almost ran over it. As it crouched in the road, the men got out of the car and encircled it. They got very close to it before one man threw a stone and the creature walked away into the forest. They noticed that it had eyes like a human's, which did not reflect the light.[9] Later that same month, two teenage girls cutting firewood saw a female man-beast with a male child. She threw him across a ditch which was too wide for him to cross alone. Shown pictures of various animals, the girls chose a gorilla as being closest to what they had seen.[10]

Gong Yulan, a peasant woman living at Qiaoshang Commune in Hubei Province was collecting grass for her pigs, on 19 June 1976, when she saw a strange red-haired creature rubbing its back against a tree (see photograph below). Later, investigators collected hairs from the tree trunk for analysis and were able to state that Gong Yulan had not seen a bear but may have seen some kind of primate, though the creature she described did not sound like any of the monkeys in the region.[11] A year later, on 6 June 1977, Pang Gensheng saw a 'hairy-man' while cutting wood in Dadi Gulley, in the Qinling area of

Here in Shennongjia forestry region, China, Gong Yulan (woman by tree) saw a 'wild man' on 19 June 1976.

Shaanxi Province. He backed up against a rock face and was stuck there for an hour or so, facing the 'hairy-man'. Although he held an axe, Pang did not use it to scare off the creature. Instead he threw a rock which injured the creature, causing it to retreat. It did not retaliate against its attacker, despite its size and strength. Pang described it as about 7 feet (2.1 metres) tall, with broad shoulders, long arms and large hands, and it had a 5-foot (1.5 metre) stride.[12]

A few weeks later, on 21 July 1977, Yang Wanchun also saw a 'hairy-man' at the same place. Although the creature was aware of the man's presence, he kept approaching until the two stood only 6 feet (1.8 metres) apart, separated by a drain.

While we were facing each other, the hairy-man uttered 11 or 12 different sounds, which seemed to imitate a sparrow chirping, dog barking, pony neighing, leopard growling and an infant crying. He changed his call incessantly for over one hour. Finally, I retreated a few steps, grabbed a stone and threw it at the hairy-man's chest. He cried out and ran toward the southeast, muttering as he went. He ascended the slope of the hill pretty rapidly by holding onto branches of trees . . . This creature was roughly 7 *chi* tall [8 feet/2.3 metres], the shoulders were 3 *chi* broad [3 feet/1 metre]. The front limbs were 3 *chi*, stretching beyond the kneecap. The head was larger than a man's, with the hair draped untidily over the shoulders. The brow hair was shorter, partly covering the forehead. His orbital ridge was high, and the eyes were sunken. His back limbs were thick-set, the thighs were particularly large. The knee joints did not appear to be very supple when he walked. The feet were similar to a man's: broad in the front and narrow behind, about 1 *chi* and 2 *cun* long [16 inches/40 centimetres]. From the imprints made on the muddy ground, we could see that the toenails were pretty deep with the five toes separated. It was tailless, and very obviously a male animal. I have been a hunter since the age of 14. I have seen most of the animals in the jungle, and this is definitely not a black bear, golden monkey, *zongyang* nor giant panda![13]

Although Yang Wanchun's description contains similarities to descriptions of Bigfoot and man-beasts elsewhere, two dissimilarities should be noted: we do not remember ever reading of a man-beast footprint showing clear toenail imprints; and, at least in North America, male man-beasts do not have noticeable genitals, as Yang Wanchun suggests his 'hairy-man' had.

Sightings have continued into the 1980s, and the scientific efforts to identify the 'wild men' also continue. Hypotheses include genetic throwbacks (hairy humans rejected by society – but would they be so tall, and so many of them around the world?), Gigantopithecus (the

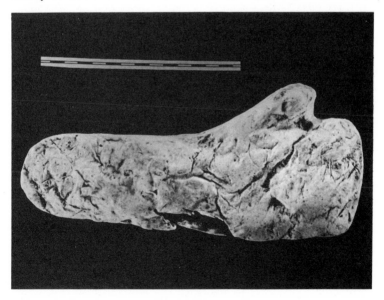

A cast of a footprint found in Tielu Gully, Shennongjia forestry region, China, on 30 August 1977.

prehistoric ape-man which lived in the mountain range where the Shennongjia forest is), and native monkeys. Four species of monkeys are known to live in the Shennongjia forest region, the golden langur, the red-faced macaque, the 'great green monkey', and the white-headed langur, but all are fairly small, and in other ways differ from the wild-man descriptions. For example, monkeys have tails, whereas a number of witnesses specifically said that the creature they saw was tailless.

Despite the many difficulties, some people remain confident of the eventual success of the scientists. The Shanghai newspaper *Wen Hui Bao* reported: 'In our country, with our superior socialist system, with the support of the Communist Party and with our legions of scientific workers devoted to the task, the secret of the wild men of Shennongjia will certainly be revealed soon.'[14]

Australian man-beasts

Whereas in China scientific expeditions are openly searching for the man-beasts and reporting the results of their searches, in Australia the approach is much more muted, and indeed it would appear that any suggestion of man-beasts inhabiting the continent is an embarrassment to the scientific community. The reports which are published come from the press and amateur investigators. However, since it is a continent only recently entered by the white man, with vast areas of uninhabited territory including forests and mountains, it would, on the strength of the evidence from elsewhere in the world, be strange if no man-beast reports had emerged from Australia. The earliest known sighting by white men dates from 1795, when a group of kangaroo hunters saw a 'giant hairy beast' near Sydney Cove in New South Wales. During the nineteenth and early twentieth centuries, sightings were reported in the press from time to time,[15] the creature being called the Yahoo, or Hairy Man. A shepherd travelling from Tamworth to Quirindi in New South

Wales in October 1844 saw one and recorded the event in his diary:

I made a camp on a high bank of the creek, lit a fire and made myself comfortable, my dog laying down at the fire alongside me. I sat smoking my pipe as the moon rose.

About an hour later, when you could discern objects 200 yards [180 metres] from the camp, I heard a curious noise coming up the creek opposite.

One hundred yards [90 metres] away I saw him. He seemed the same as a man, only larger. He was something like a gorilla, of a dark colour and, making a roaring noise, he went away towards Top Bingara, the noise getting fainter.

Next day, the shepherd wrote:

I started at daylight, getting to Bells Mountain about 9 o'clock. Mr Bridger lived there so I stopped and had breakfast. I was telling them about the night before when they said several people had seen the hairy man about there. He was often seen in the mountains towards the Gwydir and about Mt Lindsay.[16]

Most of the reports have come from south-east Australia, mainly from New South Wales (especially the Blue Mountains) and Queensland (especially the Gold Coast area). The 1970s saw a flurry of sightings and intense media interest, which encouraged witnesses of earlier decades to report their own sightings. One such was a man who as a ten-year-old boy in 1935 was living on his grandfather's farm at South Lismore, New South Wales. It was about 9 o'clock on a moonlit night in winter.

I was standing on the verandah of the farm when I thought I saw a man walking across the paddock from the direction of the hills. I remember that as it walked towards the house my grandfather's horse started to kick up a hell of a fuss in its yard. I went inside and told my grandfather that someone was coming.

When he came outside and saw what it was he pushed me inside, blew out the lamp in the living room, then grabbed his rifle. My grandparents then took me into the kitchen and we all watched through a small window as the creature walked past the house . . . its head didn't seem to have a neck, but was sitting straight on its shoulders. It also looked as if it had a hunched back, but it was standing up straight. It was much thicker around the shoulders and chest than a man.

After walking past the house it hesitated for a few seconds near the sulky shed, then kept on walking. My grandfather thought it was going to go into the shed. We lost sight of the animal when it disappeared behind the dairy. My grandfather said that it was gone and wouldn't come back.

My grandfather told me it was the same creature he had seen up in a gully on the property only a few years earlier. He said he had ridden into the gully to pick some guavas when he saw the creature come down one side of the gully, cross a small creek, then climb up the other side of the hill. I remember him telling me that his horse had played up on him very badly when the creature came into view. My grandfather said not to talk about what we had seen because people would not believe me.[17]

A selection of reports from the 1970s will confirm that the creature being seen, today known as the Yowie, bears a close resemblance to the North American Bigfoot, both in its appearance and its behaviour. Five bushwalkers in the thick bush of Grose Valley near Katoomba, New South Wales, suddenly came face to face with a female Yowie on 13 April 1976. They estimated that it stood 8 feet (2.4 metres) tall, and was 4 feet (1.2 metres) across the shoulders. Pendulous breasts showed through the dark brown hair covering the body. Men and beast stared at each other from a distance of only a few feet, but the Yowie showed no signs of attacking them. The men noticed a foul smell, a typical feature of Bigfoot reports.[18]

In 1976, hikers in the Ruined Castle area of the Jamieson Valley had unexpected meetings with the

Yowies. Mr Jackson's encounter took place in July, when he came face-to-face with a tall, hair-covered manlike creature. 'I could see his facial features clearly, almost human-like – there was a look of inquisitiveness in his face. He suddenly leaped off the track and disappeared down the embankment and into the trees.' Two months later, Ian Mack and Donald Huston heard strange noises while sitting by their campfire at night. Suddenly four 'hairy, manlike, apelike' beasts appeared, but they quickly disappeared again when the boys moved. These creatures were only about 5 feet (1.5 metres) tall, maybe young Yowies on a night-time excursion.[19]

Early in 1977, a huge black furry creature was thought to be responsible for the blood-curdling screams heard by families living on Oxley Island, a river island near Taree, New South Wales. Mrs Gee saw the creature standing on the end of a jetty waving its arms, and said it looked like an enormous ape. Footprints were also found, and a strong smell was noticed.[20] Also in 1977, a housewife in Woodenbong, New South Wales, had a rather more frightening experience when she awoke to find her terrier dog being crushed to death by an apelike creature. When it saw her, it dropped the dog, made some deep grunting noises, and ran off. This witness also noticed a strong smell coming from the Yowie. In the daylight, a footprint 9 inches (22 centimetres) long was found in the garden, and gingery-brown hair stuck to a post which the Yowie had brushed past.[21]

Early in 1978, a National Parks worker had a typical encounter with a Yowie around 7 feet (2 metres) tall. He was cutting timber in the Springbrook area of the Queensland Gold Coast when he heard a grunting noise. Thinking a pig was loose, he went into the forest to look for it.

Then something made me look up and there, about 12 feet [3.6 metres] in front of me, was this big black hairy man-thing. It looked more like a gorilla than anything. It had huge hands and one of them was wrapped around a sapling. It had a flat, black shiny face, with two big yellow eyes and a hole for a mouth. It just stared at me and I stared back. I was so numb I couldn't even raise the axe I had in my hand. We seemed to stand there staring at each other for about 10 minutes before it suddenly gave off a foul smell that made me vomit – then it just made off sideways and disappeared.

This experience convinced the witness that the Yowie is not just a myth, and he commented that they are not seen more often because people out bushwalking usually make a noise, which alerts the Yowies to their presence. He was walking quietly since he was, so he thought, stalking a pig.[22]

The American Bigfoot sometimes shows an interest in, or antipathy towards, road vehicles, a characteristic not recorded in Asia because of the absence of vehicles in the wilder terrain. Australia being a Westernized country, with a higher concentration of vehicles, the opportunities for the Yowies to encounter vehicles are naturally greater. When a Yowie came to Emerald in April 1979, leaving footprints 8.5 inches (21 centimetres) long, it was Vic the plasterer who had the misfortune to experience the creature's curious and maybe even playful nature. Vic drove to a creek bed for some purpose unknown, and while there heard noises 'like an elephant in galoshes' coming from the bush. He ran for his car, but was unable to get it moving. Feeling the car bouncing up and down, he turned and saw through the rear window two black arms and a big chest. Vic put the car into reverse, knocked the creature down, and was then able to escape. When he arrived home he found two huge muddy handprints on the back of the car.[23] Also in 1979, the Yowie reports were scaring truck-drivers and holiday-makers on the Newell Highway between Coonabarabran and Narrabri in New South Wales. They were too scared to stop and sleep by the roadside, after reports of large footprints seen by the road, and of truck drivers having their loads interfered with as they slept.[24]

Probably fear was also responsible for sixteen-year-old Warren Christensen's reaction to an encounter with the unknown. He was pig hunting and camping with seventeen-year-old Tony Solano near Kilcoy, which is north of Brisbane in Queensland. While camped in a gully beside a creek, they heard thumping noises like heavy footsteps, and went to investigate. Warren saw 'the outline of something very large protruding from behind a tree', and his immediate reaction was to draw his gun. 'I fired my .22 from the hip. It was a gut reaction – not something I would have done if I'd had time to think about it. By the time I'd ejected the cartridge and looked up again the thing had vanished.' The boys found 12-inch-long (30 centimetres) footprints in the soft sand, and the prints were apparently three-toed, an inexplicable feature which is reported from time to time in North America. The next day they found more prints at other points along the creek, and they estimated that the creature's stride was about 3 feet (1 metre). Warren asked his school biology teacher to visit the site, and she, too, saw the prints.[25]

In May 1981, three boys had a close sighting of two Yowies in isolated hill country west of Dunoon, New South Wales. The boys, aged eleven, thirteen and fourteen, were bushwalking when a hairy manlike creature crossed the path ahead of them at a distance of 20-25 feet (6-8 metres). Soon afterwards a second creature appeared. It

seemed to stumble, stopped behind a tree standing on the left side of the path, and peeped around the tree towards us. It kind of squatted behind the tree on its legs and looked at us for about five seconds before running across the path behind the other animal, which had its back towards us and appeared to be waiting for its mate to catch up.

The boys could hear the two making their way through

the thick scrub. One of the boys told how his dog reacted:

When I first saw the creature my dog went berserk. He made a sort of a crying sound as though he were having a bit of a whinge. He then chased after them down the track for a bit before we called him back, then he sniffed around in circles where the animal had crouched behind the tree.

The boys agree that the creatures they saw were about 5 feet (1.5 metres) tall, with long brownish hair all over their bodies. They appeared to have no necks, but rounded heads which 'seemed to just sit on their shoulders'. They were not wild pigs, nor wallabies, nor gorillas. The eldest boy commented: 'Gorillas are black and bow-legged. These had straight legs and were brown, more human-like.'

If these boys were lying, they did it well. The mother of the oldest boy, Craig Hatherell, said that the boys would not make up such a story, and that Craig was definitely not lying. 'I could tell just by looking at Craig and the excited way in which he described the experience that he was telling the truth. I can tell when he is lying because he can't keep a smirk off his face.' Also, there are details in their story which tie in with other reports from other parts of the world – the apparent absence of a neck, the Yowies' timid behaviour, the dog's reaction. The boys would be unlikely to have sufficient knowledge of man-beast lore to make their story sound so convincing. Also they did not hesitate to admit that they had been afraid. 'Whatever we saw up there was really scary. It was like nothing any of us have seen before.[26]

If the Australian scientists really knew anything about the subject they could not reject out of hand this convincing sighting and others like it. In 1976 Dr H. J. Frith, Chief of the CSIRO Division of Wildlife Research, commenting on reports of Yowies, said, 'There is no such animal. Some responsible person would have seen it by now. The whole thing is far-fetched.'[27] In 1977 Professor B. Rigsby, professor of anthropology at Queensland University, said that he regarded sightings of Yowies in Australia as 'highly improbable'. 'There is no reliable recurrable evidence for Yowies, abominable snowmen, yetis, big foots or wild men of the woods or whatever they are called. I believe you simply won't find a human primate of this sort in Australia.'[28] Faced with such dogmatism, the amateurs have no choice but to carry on alone, as Rex Gilroy has done for twenty-five years. He has collected over 3,000 sighting reports, and has even had two brief sightings of his own.[29] In the late 1970s he formed the Australian Yowie Research Centre, based at Katoomba, New South Wales.

The early Yowie reports have been explained away as tame monkeys allowed to run wild in the Blue Mountains by early settlers. These may indeed account for a few sightings of smaller creatures, but could hardly be valid for the most convincing of the recent reports, such as that from the Dunoon boys. Rex Gilroy suggests that the Yowie is related to Gigantopithecus and came over to Australia in prehistoric times via a land-bridge which could have existed then. There may be only 400-500 left in Australia.

Having written about the North American, Australian and part of the Asian continents, there still remain two huge continents, South America and Africa, plus central America and South-east Asia, from all of which have come man-beast reports. Unfortunately data from these areas is sparser, many of them not having been closely investigated, mainly because of problems of accessibility. But all the signs are that Europe is the only continent lacking a twentieth-century population of hairy man-beasts (though even from Europe comes the occasional tantalizingly vague report). We will complete our world round-up of man-beasts with a lightning tour of the continents so far passed by.

South-east Asian man-beasts

South of China are six countries, Burma, Thailand, Laos, Vietnam and Cambodia, with Malaya at the southern tip of a long peninsula. Northern Burma is close to some of the man-beast territories described earlier, and there have long been persistent reports of monsters in that area, especially where Burma, Thailand and Laos meet. A fairly recent report dates from 1969, when two 10-foot (3 metres) 'monkey men' with khaki-coloured hair were seen in the jungle along the Mekong River. Hunters who saw them in the Taimilek area ran away without using their weapons. They were also seen by farmers in the fields at night, and by guerillas, who had a rock thrown at them.[30]

The whole area south of China is mountains and tropical forests, much of it not yet properly explored, and it is quite feasible that man-beasts could be living there, as the intermittent reports of sightings and footprints indicate. An American soldier stationed in Vietnam saw a set of giant footprints from the air, and landed to get a closer look. Lt. Alan Szpila reported that they were about 18 inches (45 centimetres) long and 8 inches (20 centi-metres) wide. They were deeply embedded, and their maker had a 4-foot (1.2 metre) stride.[31] A giant footprint was also found by two American journalist-adventurers who in 1971 ventured into the jungle of northern Johore (Malaya) in search of man-beasts. Harold Stephens and Kurt Rolfes found an 18-inch (45 centimetre) human-like footprint far up the Endau River, and their research convinced them of the man-beast's existence.[32]

There have been occasional sightings in Malaya. On Christmas Day 1953 a Chinese girl tapping rubber trees in south Perak state was frightened by a smelly, hairy creature which crept up behind her and placed its hand on her shoulder. She said he was white-skinned, had long black head hair and a moustache, and wore a brief loincloth made of bark. She also saw two others standing some distance away near the river. The authorities were alerted and some men of the Malaya Security Guard went to the scene, where they, too, saw the creatures. As the men took out their guns, the man-beasts swam across the river and disappeared into the jungle. Next day a Hindu Indian worker on the estate had an even closer encounter. While squatting down at his work, two hairy arms embraced him. He broke free and ran away, but fainted on the way. When he came to, he saw the three creatures standing laughing at him.[33] An intriguing feature of these reports is that the creatures had white skins. Ivan T. Sanderson noted that this was always the case with reports from the Malayan region, and in his magazine *Pursuit* gave another example which he had received from an Australian who had been stationed at Seleter R.A.F. base in Malaya. On a solitary outing by canoe, he was eating fruit in a quiet spot near the beach when he was amazed to see a strange creature, not an ape and not a human, step out from the brush.

From what I saw, it was as near human as could be, large, ungainly proportioned, white yet pinkish coloured skin which was 'sparsely' covered, even the face, with long, fine, silky, fair hair. The facial skin was flabby and loose looking. The eyes seemed watery and sad looking, possibly because the lower lids sagged somewhat, and I swear the eyes were bluey-grey. If it wasn't for all that hair, its cry, and the way it rushed away, I would have supposed the local ugly man was going for a nude swim too. Male? Female? I don't know.[34]

Sumatra, which is separated from peninsular Malaysia by the Strait of Malacca, has produced persistent reports of a man-beast for centuries, and there have been several reliable twentieth-century sightings. The creature is known as Orang Pendek (little man) or Sedapa, and according to the natives it is not a gibbon or a orangutan. It is relatively small, from 2 feet 6 inches to 5 feet tall

(0.75-1.5 metres). It has short dark hair over a pinkish-brown skin, with a bushy mane down its back. It is bipedal, but is said to walk with its feet reversed, heels pointing forward. Its diet consists of young shoots, fruit, fresh-water molluscs, snakes and worms, and it sometimes raids plantations of bananas and sugar-cane, as well as native gardens.[35]

In 1923, a Dutch settler named Van Herwaarden saw a Sedapa while pig-hunting in the forest. He had already heard about the creature and talked to the local people about it, and when he found that his hunting was not proving successful he decided to sit quietly in the hope of seeing a Sedapa. His luck was in, for he saw one in a tree, and he was able to study it closely. He noted its long dark head hair, almost to its waist, its brown face with bushy eyebrows, dark lively human-like eyes, broad nose, wide mouth, humanlike ears, long arms and short legs. It was around 5 feet (1.5 metres) tall. His report continued:

There was nothing repulsive or ugly about its face, nor was it at all ape-like, although the quick nervous movements of its eyes and mouth were very like those of a monkey in distress. I began to talk in a calm and friendly way to the *sedapa*, as if I was soothing a frightened dog or horse; but it did not make much difference. When I raised my gun to the little female I heard a plaintive 'hu-hu', which was at once answered by similar echoes in the forest nearby.

I laid down my gun and climbed into the tree again. I had almost reached the foot of the bough when the *sedapa* ran very fast out along the branch, which bent heavily, hung on to the end and then dropped a good 10 feet [3 metres] to the ground. I slid hastily back to the ground, but before I could reach my gun again, the beast was almost 30 yards [27 metres] away. It went on running and gave a sort of whistle. Many people may think me childish if I say that when I saw its flying hair in the sights I did not pull the trigger. I suddenly felt that I was going to commit murder. I lifted my gun to my shoulder again, but once more my courage failed me. As far as I could see, its feet were broad and short, but that the *sedapa* runs with its heels foremost is quite untrue.[36]

Reports have also come from Borneo, where John MacKinnon, who was there to study the orangutan, saw 6-inch (15 centimetre) footprints with narrow heels,[37] and there is every likelihood that other islands, of which there are many in this area south of China between the Indian and Pacific Oceans, also provide a suitable environment for an as yet unrecognized man-beast. Or more likely man-beasts, as it must be clear from reading the reports in these two chapters of our world survey that there are certainly several different types.

Japan, New Zealand and the Arctic

Further north in the Pacific Ocean lies Japan, which despite its emphasis on industrialization still retains plenty of remote areas. The countryside around Mt. Hiba is wild, and it was there that the 'Hiba-gon monster' was reported early in the 1970s. At first it was attacking wild game on the mountain, but later it began approaching farming villages and was thought to be responsible for the disappearance of cattle and even villagers. Yokio Sazawa was digging wild sweet potatoes in the foothills of Mt. Hiba when he saw the monster: 'All of a sudden, this thing stood before me. It was about five feet [1.5 metres] tall, with a face shaped like an inverted triangle, covered with bristles, having a snub nose and large, deep, glaring eyes.' He was certain it was not a monkey. Albert Kubo saw the monster while spreading fertilizer on his rice fields. It was standing on a path, and appeared to be holding a small paper bag. Not knowing who or what it was, Kubo approached the figure.

He seemed to be lost in thought or puzzled . . . I was just about to say something when I realized it was the Hiba-gon. I was petrified, but the stench was what really got to me. He must have bathed in a septic tank and dried off with cow dung. I nearly passed out. Luckily enough, though, I managed to turn and run before it realized I was there. I ran five miles [8 kilometres] straight home without ever looking back over my shoulder.[38]

Since the Hiba-gon monster never made any move to attack the people who saw it from close to, it is doubtful whether it really was responsible for all the disappearances of cattle and people that were ascribed to it by a nervous local populace. Equally doubtful is the explanation for the monster's presence in the Hiroshima area, which was widely publicized: that it was created by radioactive fallout from the atomic bomb. The few reliable details we have of this man-beast suggest that it is just another Bigfoot-type creature, perhaps only one of many roaming Japan's mountains.

The mountains of New Zealand are also thought to hide a man-beast, the Moehau monster or Coromandel Man. The creature is said to live in the Coromandel peninsula east of Auckland on North Island, and periodically expeditions set out to look for it, so far without success.[39] We doubt if expeditions have ventured into the Arctic to search for the Toonijuk, as the man-beasts of Baffin Island, Greenland and the Canadian Arctic islands were known. We do not have any recent sighting reports, but their existence was part of Eskimo lore during the last century and into the present century. Katherine Scherman saw Toonijuk relics and heard the Eskimo lore when she visited the Arctic in the 1950s. The Toonijuk were said to be timid, not at all dangerous, and to be the remains of a primitive race of people.[40] Perhaps a few of them still survive hidden away in the (to us) inhospitable coastal valleys of Greenland and the many islands north of Canada.

African man-beasts

A book of almost 700 pages has been devoted to the man-beasts of Africa, but unfortunately for the English-speaking world it is at present only available in French – Dr Bernard Heuvelmans' *Les Bêtes Humaines d'Afrique*. Again there is no doubt that unknown creatures can and probably do exist in the depths of darkest Africa. Only recently (1981) have expeditions returned from the Congo, where they unsuccessfully sought conclusive proof of the existence of Mokele-Mbembe, possibly a small dinosaur. Ivan Sanderson noted[41] that man-beasts are mainly reported from three areas: 'the southern face of the Guinea Massif; the east side of the Congo Basin; and the eastern escarpment of Tanganyika [now united with Zanzibar as Tanzania].' The most persistent reports are of the Agogwe, little hairy men around 4 feet (1.2 metres) tall. Captain William Hichens may have seen them earlier this century:

Some years ago I was sent on an official lion-hunt to this area [Ussure and Simbiti forests on the western side of the Wembare plains] and, while waiting in a forest glade for a man-eater, I saw two small, brown, furry creatures come from dense forest on one side of the glade and disappear into the thickets on the other. They were like little men, about 4 feet [1.2 metres] high, walking upright, but clad in russet hair. The native hunter with me gazed in mingled fear and amazement. They were, he said, *agogwe*, the little furry men whom one does not see once in a lifetime. I made desperate attempts to find them, but without avail in that wellnigh impenetrable forest. They may have been monkeys, but, if so, they were no ordinary monkeys, nor baboons, nor colobus, nor Sykes, nor any other kind found in Tanganyika, What were they?[42]

Mr Cuthbert Burgoyne also saw the Agogwe.

In 1927 I was with my wife coasting Portuguese East Africa in a

Japanese cargo boat. We were sufficiently near to land to see objects clearly with a glass of 12 magnifications. There was a sloping beach with light bush above upon which several dozen baboons were hunting for and picking up shell fish or crabs, to judge by their movements. Two pure white baboons were amongst them. These are very rare but I had heard of them previously. As we watched, two little brown men walked together out of the bush and down amongst the baboons. They were certainly not any known monkey and yet they must have been akin or they would have disturbed the baboons. They were too far away to see in detail, but these small human-like animals were probably between 4 and 5 feet [1.2-1.5 metres] tall, quite upright and graceful in figure. At the time I was thrilled as they were quite evidently no beast of which I had heard or read. Later a friend and big game hunter told me he was in Portuguese East Africa with his wife and three hunters, and saw a mother, father, and child, of apparently a similar animal species, walk across the further side of a bush clearing. The natives loudly forbade him to shoot.[43]

Dr Bernard Heuvelmans suggests that the Agogwe may be surviving examples of Australopithecus, a 4-foot (1.2 metres) creature proportioned like a man and known to have lived in Africa around 500,000 years ago. It is always thought to have been destroyed by man in prehistoric times, but why should they have allowed themselves to be exterminated or superseded? It is more likely that they took to the forests, and there have survived to the present day.[44]

The man-beasts of Africa rarely receive media publicity, but in 1978 the world's press carried reports of Dr Jacqueline Roumeguere Eberhardt's work on the creatures of Kenya which she has named 'X'. A lecturer at the French National Council of Scientific Research in Paris, Dr Eberhardt has researched deeply into Masai tribesmen's reports of unidentified forest-dwelling hominoids. She has recorded five types of 'X':

X-1 is the big blond who picked up a sheep and gently examined it over his head before the terrified 17-year-old [who had been kidnapped in 1960 by the creature, which had matted blond hair, a low forehead, and wide toes with human-like toenails]. He had a large spiked club made from a hard root for catching buffalo. He has been reported by 31 adults and two children in eight forests.

X-2 has been seen by 12 persons in five forests. He is said to be hairless and white and to roam the forests only at night, letting out a piercing scream.

X-3 has been reported by five persons in one forest. He is very tall and black, with white hair trailing to his heels. He has been seen spiking buffalo through the forehead with a club or bringing them down by breaking a foreleg. He drinks blood from the jugular vein of the downed beast and leaves the rest of it, which sometimes has been taken by villagers.

X-4 has a large head and has been seen with a naked female and three children who ate tubers, berries, and mushrooms.

X-5 is similar to X-4 but carries a bow and arrow, indicating that he eats meat. He appears to be the most developed.

X-5 took to the trees when surprised by seven Masai, who took his bow and quiver of arrows, which Dr Eberhardt showed at her press conference. The Masai also took X-5's leather bags for nettle-collecting and honey storage. Dr Eberhardt was, at the time of her press conference in 1978, planning an expedition. 'The herders know only the fringe of the forest. The forest dwelling groups go in only a little farther, but we will have to go in deep and sleep in the forest if we are to make contact. I already have been assured of the co-operation of the best possible guides.'[45] We have heard no more of Dr Eberhardt and await the report of her expedition with interest. Dr Richard

Leakey, director of Kenya's National Museums, was sceptical, suggesting that the Masai tales were no more than myths, similar to those found in the lore of North American Indians. He was referring, of course, to Bigfoot, that 'myth' which leaves giant footprints.

South American man-beasts

After the wealth of man-beast lore uncovered in most of the continents, it is a surprise to learn from Ivan Sanderson that there is not much relating to South America.[46] He mentions in his book *Abominable Snowmen: Legend Come to Life* a few hints and rumours, but of solid evidence, such as first-hand sighting reports, there is little, when compared with that from the other continents. This may be simply because little research or investigation into man-beasts has been carried out in South America. When someone does make an effort to penetrate a remote area and ask about man-beasts, they are likely to find a living tradition, as was the case in Argentina recently. In 1979 anthropologist Silvia Alicia Barrios visited the mountainous regions of northern Argentina and heard about 'a strange monkey' called the Ucumar or Ucu. Don Pepe, who lives on the Argentina/Bolivia border and knows the countryside well, described the Ucu:

The Ucu lives in the hills, there in back of El Chorro [the mountainous zone with tropical vegetation], and likes to scream at the cows and chickens. It's a 'zuncho' [robust and bulky] animal and even though it doesn't run a lot, it's very strong. It's never come close to me but it has some of my countrymen. I've seen Ucus, and Ucus trapping people. If the Ucu catches someone, the best thing to do is to urinate because then it will let go. The Ucu likes to eat payo, the plant whose inside is similar to cabbage. It's big, the size of a fleecy dog, and always walks erect.[47]

The noise they make sounds like *uhu, uhu, uhu,* which

interestingly agrees with what Ivan Sanderson has written about the noise made by the Maricoxi (see later) – *Eugh, Eugh, Eugh,* or *OOgh, OOgh, OOgh* – which Sanderson compared with the *Ugh, Ugh, Ugh* reported by Albert Ostman who claimed to have been held captive by a family of Bigfeet in British Columbia in 1924.[48]

Further north, in Paraguay, there were strange reports around 1950 of cattle (a hundred at a time) found dead with their tongues torn out and gone. This happened on several occasions over several years, in the Ybitimi region. As both Heuvelmans and Sanderson remark, it is hard to explain these events, in view of the fact that both a humanlike hand and a massive strength would be needed to pull out cattle tongues.[49]

In the south-west of Brazil, particularly the provinces of Amazonas, Matto Grosso and Goyaz, and on the Bolivian frontier, the man-beast is known as the Mapinguary, while in 1914 the explorer Col. P. H. Fawcett, who later disappeared in Brazil, encountered a group of strange people called by the natives the Maricoxi. He was on an expedition from Bolivia into south-west Matto Grosso, and they were moving through uninhabited forest when they saw the 'savages'. Col. Fawcett wrote:

On catching sight of us they stopped dead and hurriedly fixed arrows to their bows, while I shouted to them in the Maxubi tongue. We could not see them clearly for the shadows dappling their bodies, but it seemed to me they were large, hairy men, with exceptionally long arms, and with foreheads sloping back from pronounced eye ridges, men of a very primitive kind, in fact, and stark naked. Suddenly they turned and made off into the undergrowth.

A day later the men came upon a village of primitive shelters, where 'great apelike brutes' were squatting making arrows, or just idling.

I whistled, and an enormous creature, hairy as a dog, leapt to his feet in the nearest shelter, fitted an arrow to his bow in a flash, and came up dancing from one leg to the other till he was only four yards [3.6 metres] away. Emitting grunts that sounded like 'Eugh! Eugh! Eugh!' he remained there dancing, and suddenly the whole forest around us was alive with these hideous ape-men, all grunting 'Eugh! Eugh! Eugh!' and dancing from leg to leg in the same way as they strung arrows to their bows. It looked like a very delicate situation for us, and I wondered if it was the end. I made friendly overtures in Maxubi, but they paid no attention. It was as though human speech were beyond their powers of comprehension.

Twice the man-beast at the front raised his bow but did not shoot. The third time, Fawcett knew he would shoot, so he took out his pistol and fired into the ground.

The effect was instantaneous. A look of complete amazement came into the hideous face, and the little eyes opened wide. He dropped his bow and arrow and sprang away as quickly as a cat to vanish behind a tree. Then the arrows began to fly. We shot off a few rounds into the branches, hoping the noise would scare the savages into a more receptive frame of mind, but they seemed in no way disposed to accept us, and before anyone was hurt we gave it up as hopeless and retreated down the trail till the camp was out of sight.

Col. Fawcett was told of other groups of primitive peoples living in the area. Ivan Sanderson, who wrote of the Maricoxi in his book *"Things"*,[50] concluded: 'The only final conclusion we can therefore draw is, I contend, an acceptance of the fact that there were neanderthaloid-type Submen living in the Matto Grosso in 1914. There is no reason to suppose that they are not still living there.'
    Within the last 10 years, press reports originating in Lima, Peru, suggested that there may still be 'stone age giants' living in the northern jungles of that country.

Explorer Carlos Torrealza claimed to have discovered the giants while he was lost in the jungle during April 1976. The encounter took place in thick rain-forest in San Martin province, east of the Andes. Torrealza said the men were olive-skinned, barefoot and hunchback, more than 6 feet 6 inches (1.9 metres) tall, had red hair and wore animal skins. An Indian guide, Encarnacion Napuri, reported at around the same time that a group of fifteen giants had attacked a camp of professional hunters.[51]

In the north of the continent, especially Venezuela, there have been persistent reports of the Didi, a short and powerful wild man covered with hair, as far back as the eighteenth century, and several encounters have been recorded. In 1769 Dr Edward Bancroft wrote of an 'orangutan' in Guiana

much larger than either the *African* [the chimpanzee] or *Oriental*, if the accounts of the natives may be relied on... They are represented by the *Indians* as being near five feet [1.5 metres] in height, maintaining an erect position, and having a human form, thinly covered with short black hair; but I suspect that their height has been augmented by the fears of the *Indians*, who greatly dread them...[52]

At the end of that century the explorer Alexander von Humboldt returned from the Upper Orinoco having heard tales of a hairy man-beast. In 1910 a Mr Haines, later a British Resident Magistrate in British Guiana, actually saw two of them while prospecting for gold along the Konawaruk. They had human features and were covered with reddish-brown fur. They did not attack the apprehensive man, who was himself unarmed, but retreated slowly into the forest, probably as surprised as he was.[53]

More recently, Pino Turolla reported a brief encounter with man-beasts while he was in Venezuela engaged in archaeological exploration. His guide Antonio had described his own encounter with El Mono Grande, and

Turolla asked if they could visit the place. They heard howling and crashing noises as they entered the canyon, and the Indians accompanying them turned and fled. Advancing slowly, Turolla glimpsed two furry creatures at the far end of a clearing. He saw them only briefly as they disappeared into the jungle, but saw that they were over 5 feet (1.5 metres) tall, hairy, apelike, yet moving on two legs.[54]

Even more dramatic was Emelino Martinez's story of his fight with two hairy man-beasts on 10 April 1954. He claimed that they followed him as he returned to his car after a hunting trip in the Venezuelan hills, and that they grabbed him as he was just about to get into the car. They fought, and Martinez managed to hit one of the creatures on the head with a rock, before escaping in his car with the two pounding their fists on the windows. Although violent behaviour has sometimes been recorded, it is so contrary to the man-beast's normal reaction on seeing humans that we would be wise to treat such stories with caution, despite in this case the additional information that blood found on leaves at the site could not be identified.[55]

In central America, Guatemala and Belize are the two countries from which have emerged rumours of man-beasts. In Belize the creatures living in the wet forests are known as Dwendis (from Spanish *duende*, goblin). The Dwendis are small, with long arms, covered all over with thick, short brown hair, and have flat, yellowish faces. They are quiet but curious, non-violent except that they will chase and capture dogs. Ivan Sanderson lived in central America for a while and spoke to people who had seen the Dwendis.[56]

In adjoining Guatemala, reports of El Sisemite centre on Cubulco, where the terrain is forested mountains. Here are said to live hairy wild men with no necks, small eyes, long arms and big hands. Their footprints are twice as long as a man's. The strange feature of the feet pointing the wrong way in order to baffle hunters, is also attributed to El Sisemite. He is said to capture women, and there is a story that, probably during the last century, a woman was taken by one and lived with him for many years before being captured by hunters and returned to her husband. He could not recognize her, and she refused to speak or eat, dying shortly afterwards. Although this tale was said to be factual, the woman who told it being able to remember the husband Felipe living to be an old man, it is of course impossible to be sure, without being able to speak to an actual eyewitness, where fact ends and folklore begins. One is reminded of such urban legends as the 'phantom hitchhiker', tales which travel round for decades, always told as factual stories, but very probably fictional in most cases – though some may originally have had a basis in fact, which may be the case with tales like that of El Sisemite capturing women.[57]

Our world tour ends almost on the southern border of the United States of America, to which we will now return in order to examine in detail the physical evidence there is to support the eye-witness accounts of Bigfoot, and to discuss the creature's behaviour patterns.

FOUR: MATERIAL EVIDENCE
AND BEHAVIOUR PATTERNS

I'll never forget the first one: As I dropped to my knees for a closer look at the six-inch-wide [15 centimetres] track, I wondered if this was for real or was someone playing a colossal joke on me.

Skeptically testing the stream bank near the footprint, first with my thumb and then by jumping on the ground with my treaded boots, I realized that whatever made that inch-deep [2.5 centimetres] track had to weigh far more than my 170 pounds [76 kilograms].

Again I looked at the track. Each toe was well defined: the ball of the foot behind the big toe was typical of anthropoids. Then I pulled off my boot and sock and placed my 10½B foot next to the track – only half as wide. 'It must have been Bigfoot!' I thought.[1]

The evidence for Bigfoot does not consist solely of eye-witness sighting reports. We also have more 'solid' evidence in the form of footprints, hair, faeces, tape recordings of vocalizations, and photographs. These more tangible items give the scientific researchers something to work on, and interesting conclusions have been drawn.

Footprints and tracks
Footprints have probably provided most information, as so many have been found over the years. They vary in

clarity of detail, but occasionally very good prints are found, as for example those near Walla Walla, Washington, described in Chapter 1, which show clear dermal ridges. Also convincing, and difficult if not impossible to hoax, were the Bossburg (Washington) tracks, a series of over 1,000 prints found in the snow in October 1969 and seen by researcher René Dahinden. The creature that left the tracks had a normal left foot, but its right was a club-foot, and Dr John Napier did not believe it possible that the tracks could have been hoaxed.[2]

People who do not have much knowledge of Bigfoot data often cry 'Hoax!' when tracks are found, and although it is certain that on a few occasions a hoax has been perpetrated, such events seem rare, and hoax tracks are usually easily detected. Bigfoot footprints are often found in mud or snow in isolated areas, rarely visited by humans, and who would take the trouble to perform a hoax in such a place? Hoaxers usually want their handiwork to be seen. Also, Bigfoot tracks can often be followed for some distance over awkward terrain where it would be difficult for a hoaxer to operate convincingly, and because of the creature's weight the genuine tracks are usually impressed more deeply than a hoaxer could easily manage. A hoaxer's attempt to duplicate the pressure exerted by a Bigfoot does not leave the dirt ridges that form round genuine prints. Someone who has been studying Bigfoot prints for years can easily spot hoaxes. Apart from anything else, such prints look rigid, whereas genuine prints are flexible, and in a series may show independent toe movements.

The expert on Bigfoot footprints is Grover S. Krantz, professor of anthropology at Washington State University. He writes that even though a typical Bigfoot footprint looks very similar to a man's, though increased in length to around 17 inches (43 centimetres), there are certain peculiarities in the Bigfoot tracks, caused by the creature's greater size and weight. For example, the prints show no instep or arch – Bigfoot is flat-footed. This is a direct consequence of the weight which the feet have to bear, and Professor Krantz reports that he has seen smaller tracks, perhaps those of youngsters, which do show some arching. The bulk of Professor Krantz's work on Bigfoot tracks is far too detailed for inclusion in this short book, but he has written papers which can be obtained by those having a particular interest in this aspect of Bigfoot research.[3]

Dr Grover Krantz, a professor of anthropology at Washington State University, with a cast of a Bigfoot footprint.

To the non-specialist, who does not notice and could not interpret the subtlest features of a Bigfoot footprint, the most obvious features which demonstrate its strangeness are the size and the depth. George Harrison, whose description opened this chapter, was amazed by both size

That the large mystery footprints are not usually made by bears is demonstrated by this comparison between a footprint (above) found on Blue Creek Mountain, California, in September 1967 (15 inches/38 cm long), and a bear footprint (below), 7½ inches (19 cm) long.

and depth of the print he found, and he should not have been taken by surprise as he was at the time taking part in an expedition which was looking for Bigfoot. This just illustrates how impressive the footprints are. Footprint discoveries are reported regularly, and such finds outnumber sightings of the creature itself. Obviously not all the tracks have been made by a Bigfoot. As well as hoaxes, animal tracks are sometimes misinterpreted. Although bear tracks look very different from Bigfoot tracks (see photographs on page 93), there are circumstances in which the two might possibly be confused. Footprints 12 inches (30 centimetres) long, 6 inches (15 centimetres) wide at the toes and 4 inches (10 centimetres) wide at the heel were found near Alder Dam, Thurston County, Washington, in late May 1981. But though large, the tracks did not resemble the familiar Bigfoot tracks. There was no clear big toe, the toes being all about the same size. It was decided that the prints had been made by a bear. Its back feet had landed in the prints left by its front feet, thus leaving larger tracks than normal.[4] Usually bear tracks, whether single or overlapping, are clearly distinguishable from Bigfoot tracks, unless they are very indistinct, for example in melting snow.

But indistinct tracks of any kind are not really of much use, as they can be open to almost any interpretation. It may sometimes be indistinct prints which give rise to reports of three-toed, four-toed, or even six-toed Bigfeet. Usually the prints are five-toed, but variations occur often enough to require consideration rather than dismissal. It might be possible to explain four-toed prints by saying that the little toe did not make an impression. But it is difficult to explain six-toed prints – unless it is sometimes possible for an extra toe to grow? Following the sighting of two man-beasts, one large, one small, in the northern USSR north-east of Arkhangel'sk in 1920, Bulygin Efim Ivanovich examined the creatures' footprints, and of the larger one's prints said: 'His toes were very clearly distinguishable. There were six in all and approximately of the same length. The print was very similar to that of a human being but it was flat like that of a bear and the toes were not shaped like toes of a human being but they were more splayed.'[5] It is hard to believe that there would be hoaxers around in 1920 (or at any time) in such a remote area.

The three-toed prints are the strangest, and on this puzzling topic researcher John Green has said: 'I wish there weren't any three-toed tracks, since it would simplify matters immensely... In the first place, it would be more logical for a hoaxer to put in the right number of toes. In the second place, the three-toed tracks found up in Washington last January were remarkably consistent, went on for hundreds of yards and were sunk deeply into the sand bar. I don't know whether or not the tracks were faked, but if someone did, I'd very much like to know how it was done.'[6]

So would Linda Williford, who found three-toed tracks on her rural property in Washington State. This discovery was preceded by two years of strange night-time screams, animal disturbances, and the discovery of the hide and skeleton of a large dog which had been beheaded. On 6 September 1979 Mrs Williford found some three-toed tracks impressed deeply into the hard gravel shoulder of the road. The largest was 18 inches (45 centimetres) long, 14 inches (35 centimetres) across the toes, and 11 inches (28 centimetres) across the heel. In November 1980 a child saw a large 'bear', over 6 feet (1.8 metres) tall, walking on two legs and carrying a live rabbit. That same month, only half a mile away, a boy saw a large apelike creature which stood and watched him for a while before lumbering away with its arms swinging. During 1981 the screams continued, and more three-toed tracks were found. Mrs Williford put out food for the creatures, and it, or they, would come for it. She found a three-toed print 16 inches (40 centimetres) long beside some pastry dropped by the creature. On 13 May at 5 a.m., the time when the dogs were normally disturbed, Mrs Williford kept watch and saw a massive dark form coming to take the food. Seeing her, it slowly walked away, and never came back for food.[7] This report is interesting because the three-toed prints were not just an isolated discovery. Mrs Williford found them on several occasions, while at the same time experiencing other evidence of Bigfoot's presence, such as the screams, food-stealing, and eye-witness sightings. We are certainly not knowledgeable enough to discuss the degree of likelihood or impossibility of any Bigfoot having three-toed feet, but we go along with John Green when he says of the three-toed print, 'We can't call it fake simply because it's anomalous.'

Faeces and hair samples

Not found so often as footprints, but likely to provide useful information when analysed, are faeces.[8] However, analysis cannot prove conclusively what produced the faeces, so until faeces are obtained whose production by a Bigfoot was actually witnessed, researchers cannot be sure of the source of the material they are analysing. The nearest we have got to this ideal situation seems to be William Roe's discovery of droppings which he believed to have been left by the Bigfoot he saw at close quarters on Mica Mountain in 1955. The creature was eating leaves off a bush, and afterwards Roe was curious to find out more about its diet. He said: 'I wanted to find out if it lived on vegetation entirely or ate meat as well, so I went down and looked for signs. I found it in five different places, and although I examined it thoroughly, could find no hair or shells or bugs or insects. So I believe it was strictly a vegetarian.'[9] However, not all Bigfoot droppings indicate a totally vegetarian diet, and there is plenty of other evidence to suggest that Bigfoot is omnivorous. We will give more details of Bigfoot's diet later in this chapter.

Bill Sheets of the Mammal Research Team based in Lima, Ohio, illustrates how frustrating faeces analysis can be.

They usually mark the faeces ['] unknown as human type digestive tract[']. One sample found west of Lima was sent in and the analysis revealed that the faeces contained berry seeds, and a large amount of hair, and that it came from a human type digestive tract. There was no explanation for the wood fibre that was in it. The intimation was that the sample was that of a man who lived off the wild, eating animals, hair and all, and chewing on trees.[10]

During the intensive search for wild men that took place in China during the 1970s, faeces were found and analysed. One specimen was shaped like human faeces, and contained undigested residues of fruit peels and raw millet, but no animal bones or hair. Another sample contained the skins of insect pupae. It was concluded that the droppings were from an omnivorous primate, not from a man, bear, carnivore, or ungulate.[11]

The analysis of hair samples is even more frustrating because no analyst has a definite sample of Bigfoot hair with which to compare the hairs sent for analysis. Usually all the analyst can do is report what animals the hair does *not* come from. Even that is a time-consuming business, there being so many possibilities.[12] Each animal has several different types of hair, man himself having five – head-hair, normal body hair, armpit hair, pubic hair, and fluff-like hair.[13] When Chinese scientists studied the hairs found where a wild man had rubbed himself against a tree trunk (Gong Yulan's 1976 sighting, recorded in Chapter 3), they were able to rule out a bear, but the most they could say was that the characteristics of the hair were 'relatively close to those of primates'.[14] Without some Bigfoot hair for comparison, this is as far as any hair analyst can truthfully go.

Of course the scientists would obviously prefer to have some larger portion of a Bigfoot to analyse, a complete corpse being the ideal, but failing that a head, jawbone, hand, foot, or *anything*! So far not even a finger bone has been found, and readers who question the existence of Bigfoot in the light of the complete absence of physical remains will have their question answered in Chapter 6. Suffice it to say here, that absence of evidence is not evidence of absence. In 1968 it was thought that a corpse had been located, in Minnesota where a showman was displaying what appeared to be the body of a hair-covered hominid frozen into a semi-opaque block of ice. Ivan T. Sanderson and Dr Bernard Heuvelmans examined the corpse as closely as they could, which was frustratingly difficult because of the ice, and both were convinced of its authenticity. Since then, a model seems to have been substituted, and no one knows the whereabouts of the corpse – if it really did exist.[15]

Photographic evidence: the Patterson film
It might be thought that the next best form of evidence after a corpse would be a photograph, but, as our experience of paranormal photography has shown us, photography should never be relied upon as evidence of anything, because an expert photographer can produce realistic hoaxes without too much difficulty, and so can a photographer without expert knowledge if he has luck on his side. In the Bigfoot field, there are few photographs purporting to show a living Bigfoot, and only one of these has any degree of solid support from the people who really know about Bigfoot. The photographer was the late Roger Patterson, who during the early 1960s was heavily involved in Bigfoot investigation and wrote a published book on the subject. In the autumn of 1967 he and Bob Gimlin went to Bluff Creek in California to look for Bigfoot. They travelled on horseback, following roads, tracks, and creek beds, and it was while splashing

along a creek that they came across a female Bigfoot squatting beside the water. The horses reared in alarm and Patterson scrambled off and grabbed his movie camera from his saddlebag. By now the Bigfoot was walking away across a sandbar, and Patterson had to run after it to try and get closer. At the same time he was filming, which explains why most of the resulting film is somewhat blurred. When he was about 80 feet (24 metres) away, Patterson stopped running and the Bigfoot turned to look at him. This part of the film, while the Bigfoot walked about nine paces into the trees, is the clearest, although even this part is slightly blurred, and the creature is rather dark and underexposed. Patterson and Gimlin also photographed and made casts of the creature's footprints, which were 14 inches (35 centimetres) long and 5 inches (12 centimetres) wide at the ball. They filmed the tracks, and this film shows that although the tracks were an inch deep in the hard sand, the men made little impression as they walked about.[16]

The natural reaction of many people on seeing the film, especially scientists, is to brush it off as a hoax. But there are convincing arguments against that easy explanation. The creature's build and gait are not those of a human; it has features difficult to fake (e.g. pointed head, long arms, prominent buttocks, the appropriate muscle movements, a double ball on the sole of the foot, and also good footprints were seen which were definitely left by the Bigfoot); an expert in making ape suits was impressed by the film. He said that to show muscle movement, a skin-tight suit would have to be used, not a padded suit. The experts at Disney Studios also felt that it was an effect they, with all their expertise, would not attempt to achieve.[17] When all the features are considered, it seems that if the Patterson movie was some kind of hoax, it was brilliantly done, having convinced those people who know most about the man-beast and his appearance, and so would be most likely to spot anomalies which any hoaxer

A frame from a movie film of Bigfoot taken by Roger Patterson on 20 October 1967 at Bluff Creek, northern California. The drawing (below, left) is Russian researcher Dmitri Bayanov's interpretation of the Bigfoot's head. Compare these with the photograph (below, right) of a bear standing awkwardly on its hind legs. These pictures provide visual evidence that whatever Bigfoot is, it is not a bear.

would be sure to introduce, unless he, too, were an expert on Bigfoot. The only people it doesn't convince are those who know least about the subject! It is easier to accept that the film really does show a Bigfoot.

Research and analysis of the Patterson film continue, mostly serious but with unexpected humorous facets. In 1981 Jon Beckjord, who claimed to be analysing the film, reported: 'Upon examination, we feel there exists a baby Sasquatch creature, looking like a baby monkey, hanging on for dear life to the Sasquatch Mama creature.'[18] Beckjord's interpretation was soon disputed, by Bruce Bonney who was also analysing the film, he having made the best quality prints yet produced from the film. He pointed out that when working from copy prints, or copies of copies, the images soon lose sharpness and clarity, and computer enhancement of poor quality images can be misleading. None of the scientists who have analysed the film has reported seeing a baby, and when asked in October 1981 if he had seen any such thing at the time of the filming, Bob Gimlin declared angrily: 'There was *no way on this Earth* there could have been a baby hangin' on to that creature! There was no baby! *Nothing!* There was *nothing* on this thing!' Bonney concluded that the baby 'does not exist and is merely a complex optical delusion.'[19]

Other movie films showing Bigfoot have been made, but none inspires as much confidence in its authenticity as does Roger Patterson's film. The same applies to the occasional still shot that emerges. Either extravagant claims are made by the photographer, or else the film shows nothing which could not be duplicated by a man in a gorilla suit. The question arises: Why are there not more authentic-looking photographs of Bigfoot? If he really has been seen over 1,000 times this century, wouldn't you expect that at least some of the witnesses would be equipped with cameras? It is true that sometimes witnesses do have cameras with them, but in the excitement of the moment the last thing they are thinking about is taking photographs. Rick Knovich saw a Bigfoot in Scotch Run Valley, Pennsylvania, on 18 July 1980. He stopped his car to look at something he had noticed on the railway beside the road. 'It started walking right towards the car. It was all black, with long black hair. It was walking up the railroad bed toward me.' When the creature was 50 feet (15 metres) away, Knovich grabbed his gun and startd to get out of the car. 'I had my camera right in the seat next to me, but I just didn't think to use the darn thing. I just went for my gun because the thing was coming right at me.' The creature veered off into the bush, and Knovich decided not to pursue it alone.[20]

The only person who might remember to use a camera when faced by a 7-foot (2 metre) Bigfoot would be a professional photographer to whom the camera is an extension of him- or herself and can be operated without thinking, or the dedicated Bigfoot hunter like Roger Patterson who is at all times aware of the importance of obtaining good quality evidence. Unfortunately Bigfoot hunters who venture into the wilds rarely see Bigfoot, whether they are armed with cameras or with guns. Because of its ability to see yet not be seen, and also the small number of Bigfeet thought to be still surviving (Professor Grover Krantz estimates that there are about 200-300 living in the Pacific Northwest),[21] the odds *against* anyone getting close to a Bigfoot for long enough to photograph it, always assuming that the witness has a camera ready for action, are very high. Roger Patterson was lucky. In the seventeen years since his film was made, and despite the continued sightings, no one has even come close to getting photographs as clear as Patterson's.

Vocalizations
Having discussed the tangible and visible evidence for Bigfoot, there still remains one other form of evidence: its vocalizations. There are many reports describing

Bigfoot's cry, but not all are from witnesses who saw the creature making the sound. Often the reports come from people who saw a Bigfoot and later heard the cry; or from people who suspect Bigfoot may be in the area, and the strange cries fuel their suspicions even though no Bigfoot has been seen. The noises described include grunts, growls, whistles, squeals, barks, screeches, roars, screams, whines, shrieks. Sixteen-year-old Tim Meissner, who was fishing in Dunn Lake, British Columbia, on 28 April 1979, heard a high-pitched screech lasting for about 30 seconds and, looking up, saw a Bigfoot running along the opposite edge of the lake and into the trees. Two days later he had a much closer sighting.[22]

Rich Knovich, whose 1980 sighting we mentioned earlier, heard a strange cry the night of his sighting. He was staying at his cabin (where he had been heading when he saw the Bigfoot) with relatives and they were woken by a loud, high-pitched crying sound which was not recognizable. 'It was one heck of a weird yell.' Outside they found the dogs cowering in their pens.[23]

Tom Talanca and a friend saw a Bigfoot in the same area a month after Knovich's experience, on 18 August 1980. It was standing in the middle of the road on the north side of Jonestown Mountain, Pennsylvania, but moved into the bushes when their truck appeared. They stopped, got out and followed it on foot, but after a short distance they thought better of such rash action. They could hear a dog barking, interspersed with a loud crying-like howl – 'It's a hard sound to explain.'[24]

There are, of course, plenty of natural explanations for strange sounds heard in the forests – dogs, cows, deer, bears, panthers, for example. A game warden explained one 'bone-chilling' sound, a deep bark, half-roar and half-growl, heard near Slate Run, Pennsylvania: 'Would you believe that noise was probably a big whitetail buck? When deer come across something while feeding at night, they make that barking grunt to try to scare away whatever is in their territory . . . deer aren't used to campers this time of year.'[25] But not all the strange forest sounds can be explained away as issuing from the throats of domestic or wild animals, and to prove this there have been attempts to record the sounds made by Bigfoot and get them analysed. The most notable effort was by journalist Alan Berry, who in October 1972 was camping in the High Sierras of northern California, 8 miles (13 kilometres) from the nearest trail. He was there specifically to see, photograph, tape-record, and perhaps make contact with the Bigfeet, which had already been seen in the area by the people he was camping with. He did see and hear the creatures for himself, and was able to record their whistles and chattering. When he tried to have the tapes analysed, he met the predictable 'Hoax!' reaction, but eventually the tapes were analysed by R. Lynn Kirlin and Lasse Hertel using accepted techniques of signal processing, and they concluded that 'the means and ranges of the recorded pitch and estimated vocal tract length of the speakers indicate that the sounds were made by a creature with vocal features corresponding to a larger physical size than man.' They also thought that the tape showed no signs of being pre-recorded or re-recorded at altered speed.[26]

*   *   *   *

So far as physical evidence for Bigfoot is concerned, the footprints are clearly the most productive of data, followed by Roger Patterson's movie film, and with the analysis of faeces, hair, and vocalizations contributing some additional, if somewhat inconclusive, information. All this evidence is independent of the witness accounts, which constitute the bulk of the evidence for Bigfoot. Since there are 1-2,000 reports to call on, these must reveal some consistent features and behaviour patterns which can tell us more about our quarry.

Behaviour patterns

In Chapter 1 we described the 'average' North American Bigfoot by reference to the data gleaned from sighting reports, and we will now describe the predominant behaviour patterns which have emerged. We are certainly not the first to do this. John Green, a Bigfoot researcher based in British Columbia, has been collecting Bigfoot reports for more than twenty-five years and has over 2,000 of them to call on, as against our own 'meagre' 1,000. In 1978 he published a 500-page survey of his data, *Sasquatch – The Apes Among Us*, which makes vital and exciting reading. He was able to quote statistics acquired from analysis of his own data, which revealed such things as that the average height of Bigfoot overall (from 465 cases in which height was mentioned) is 7.55 feet (2.28 metres), and that the average height of Bigfoot in California and Oregon is higher – 8.21 feet (2.45 metres) and 8.45 feet (2.58 metres) respectively.[27] John Green's survey is probably the most reliable all-round statement on Bigfoot that has yet been produced, since he has made no attempt to prove a deeply held belief but has concentrated on documenting the creature's behaviour as described by eye-witnesses.

The material which follows is based mainly on recent events that have not yet been widely reported in other books. For older reports describing similar behaviour patterns the reader should turn to our own *Bigfoot Casebook* and to John Green's *Sasquatch: The Apes Among Us*.

The most noticeable feature of Bigfoot behaviour is that he seems to prefer to keep away from human beings. Confrontations brought about by Bigfoot, other than accidentally, are rare. If Bigfoot and humankind come suddenly face to face, the Bigfoot will quietly move off into concealment. It is probable that Bigfoot is usually aware when people are around – after all, most people are not able to walk quietly through a forest, which is where a large number of sightings take place – and keeps out of sight in the undergrowth. Sightings often take place on roads or tracks passing through wooded areas, when a Bigfoot is taken by surprise by people in a car or truck, and we have already given several examples of such encounters. However, Bigfoot also has a strong streak of curiosity, or at least that is one way to explain his habit of sneaking up on unsuspecting people in the forest, usually holiday-makers or hunters camping, also loggers at work, and watching them. It may also be that he resents their intrusion into his territory, for he is sometimes not content to simply watch, but may also 'shout' at the intruders, or shake their vehicle. A party of campers left their camp in the Sitting Bull Falls area near Carlsbad, New Mexico, in October 1980 after seeing a Bigfoot. It did nothing more than walk around their camp and scream loudly, but that was enough to persuade the interlopers to move on.[28] Two men hunting near Wheeler, Oregon, in late 1979, found several large footprints, and at night their camper was shaken. Around 2 a.m. on 1 November, John Parson went outside the camper and saw a human-like figure 7½ feet (2.3 metres) tall standing in the moonlight 50 feet (15 metres) away.[29]

It is probably also curiosity or territorial protectiveness which causes Bigfoot to approach people and cars, and although this behaviour may seem frightening to the witness, the Bigfoot rarely acts violently towards humans. Considering his size and strength, he could easily kill any puny human if he felt so inclined. That he does not, demonstrates clearly his non-aggressive nature. Injury to a witness resulting from a Bigfoot encounter is more likely to be accidental, as happened on 30 August 1980 when Brian Balnap and Clynn Josephson were panning for gold on Mine Creek near Malad, Idaho. A manlike creature 9½-10 feet (2.9-3 metres) tall and covered with long dark hair walked towards them, causing them to take off on horseback. However, the horses were frightened too, and kicked and bucked. Josephson's horse rolled over, and his wrist was broken.[30] Equally frightening, but again probably not intended that way by the Bigfoot, was the experience of a woman driving at night near Julian, California. A huge hairy animal with a manlike face bounded along beside the car and tried to thrust his arm into the vehicle. She escaped by accelerating away from him.[31] There are occasional reports of Bigfoot attacking people, or at least grabbing them, as happened to Jackie Tharp during the winter of 1977 outside her home in Williams, Indiana. When she screamed, the Bigfoot let go and went away.[32] From the happy conclusion to this potentially dangerous encounter, it seems again as if the creature's motive was curiosity (or friendliness?) rather than belligerence.

Reports of fatal attacks on man are rare, and it is clear that Bigfoot does not see man as a source of food. One wonders why this should be, when he appears to be happy to kill and eat other large creatures such as deer. Farmers also blame livestock killings on Bigfoot, but apart from chicken killings there is little positive evidence to prove that Bigfoot was responsible. It is usually more likely that a big cat like a panther or puma was to blame. Bigfoot will also not miss a chance to save himself work. In 1957 a man hunting deer at Wanoga Butte near Bend, Oregon, watched in amazement as a Bigfoot made off with a deer that the hunter had just shot. In anger the hunter fired repeatedly into the Bigfoot's departing back, but the creature just kept going.[33] Whether cases like this indicate that Bigfoot has some strange invulnerability to gunfire, we shall discuss in the next chapter.

It seems clear from numerous reports over the years that Bigfoot has an antipathy towards dogs. These often cower away when Bigfoot is around and refuse to attack: wisely, judging by the fate of braver dogs. Sometimes a dog will fight to the death – its own. Sometimes a Bigfoot will merely express its dislike for dogs, as apparently happened in December 1981 in Lexington Township,

Michigan. Kathy Hensley heard her dogs barking one evening and went outside to investigate. The porch light lit up a large hairy animal over 6 feet (1.8 metres) tall which was holding her Alsatian Max. The dog was screaming, but the creature did not kill it, simply threw it for some distance. Mrs Hensley thought the animal must be a bear, but its behaviour is consistent with how Bigfoot treats dogs, and also she lives only 10 miles (16 kilometres) away from the Barone farm, where around the same time Tina Barone accidentally touched a big hairy creature in the barn.[34]

Mrs Hensley's report also demonstrates another familiar characteristic of Bigfoot behaviour: its frequent approaches to rural homes. This does not contradict our earlier statement that Bigfoot is secretive and tends to avoid humans, for he usually only visits settlements during the night. Sightings are accidental, usually brought about when his curiosity is too intense and he forgets to be cautious and draws attention to himself, perhaps by peering in at a window, or trying to open a door. Or else the dogs start barking and the occupant goes outside to investigate and sees the Bigfoot. There seem to be two main reasons why Bigfoot visits settlements – curiosity, and the search for food. It was barking dogs which woke Marie Stumbauch of Palmdale, California, early in the morning of 27 August 1980. Her eighteen-year-old son looked out of the window and saw what he thought was a large human standing in the yard. As he watched, it ran away. Afterwards footprints 9 inches (23 centimetres) long were found.[35]

The houses visited are not always isolated. Mrs Marion Dean of Artesia, New Mexico, claimed that she saw a 7 foot (2 metres) tall 'thing' covered in black fur standing in an alley near her apartment block. She went outside at 11 p.m. one night late in October 1980 when her dog was making a fuss, and saw the creature standing near a garbage container (a clue to the reason for its presence?).

She reported: 'It didn't move, it just stood still and glared at me. I unchained my dog and acted like I hadn't seen it, but I looked at it all the time.' She returned to her apartment, but when she looked out for the creature it had gone. 'But it stood there long enough for me to know I saw it. I don't know what it could be, but I would stand on a stack of Bibles and say I saw it.'[36] Both Artesia and Palmdale are sizeable towns, but both are surrounded by wild and desolate country where Bigfoot could easily live undetected.

Despite the efforts of hunters and others, Bigfoot does live largely undetected. He is secretive, and tracking is rarely successful. Footprints are often found, but they do not lead to a Bigfoot hideout. It has even been suggested that Bigfoot purposely sets out to confuse trackers by leaving tracks as rarely as possible. Hideouts or nests are never found, though it is suggested that the Bigfeet live in caves where these exist, or build nests of branches, or dig shallow beds in soft ground. There is one known report of Bigfeet seen sleeping in the open. They had their backs to the sky, and their knees and elbows were drawn up under their bodies. The same witness also later saw one of these two female Bigfeet defaecate in a creek. This sighting was made in Oregon in November 1968, and was one of several described by this witness.[37]

Several reports are on record of Bigfeet seen in water, a recent sighting being made by Jose Rivera in the San Antonio Valley, California, on 21 December 1980. Rivera was searching for three lost cows and hearing splashing from a pond ahead he got out his rifle, thinking it was wild pigs. When he got nearer, 125 feet (37 metres) away, he saw two hairy creatures, one 5 feet (1.5 metres) tall, the other 7 feet (2 metres) tall, splashing in the water. They stopped and looked at him, and he wondered whether to shoot one of them, but decided not to, and left instead.[38] Sometimes tracks are seen leading into or out of water, as on 21 April 1982 when two sets of footprints were found coming out of the Satsop River at Brady, Washington. The creatures got out of the river by climbing on a boat ramp. One set of prints measured 17 inches (43 centimetres) long by 7 inches (17 centimetres) wide, the other was 15 x 5 inches (38 x 12 centimetres). Said Deputy Dennis Heryford: 'If it was a hoax, the person went all out to do it. We had a 260-pound [117 kilogram] deputy jump next to the footprints, and he didn't make near the impression.'[39] Bigfeet have been seen swimming, which is presumably what they were doing in the Satsop River, and they might use this method to get from one place to another if the shortest route is across a river or lake. The Bigfeet seen splashing in the pond may have been playing rather than bathing. Judging from the smells reported by witnesses, Bigfoot takes baths by accident rather than by design!

Diet

The secret of Bigfoot's successful survival may lie in his ability to live largely undetected by his main enemy, man. A contributory factor would also seem to be his adaptability to whatever food is available. The accumulated reports, as well as faeces analysis, indicate that the Bigfoot eats a very wide range of food. Flesh foods include deer, birds, domestic chickens, fish, clams, rabbits, and other small creatures. One witness watched a family of Bigfeet digging among rocks for small rodents, which they then ate.[40] Another man, fishing near Hoopa, California, saw a giant hair-covered man about 10 feet (3 metres) tall standing in the water holding two salmon crosswise. In his big hands the fish looked like trout.[41] Bigfoot does sometimes kill his own deer, rather than stealing from hunters. Tim Meissner, whose sightings in British Columbia in April 1979 have already been mentioned, found a dead deer while investigating the location of his first sighting. It was unmarked except for crushed vertebrae in its neck, and it was hidden under branches, leaves, twigs and moss.[42]

Among the other foods sampled by Bigfoot are apples, berries, corn, grass, twigs and leaves, fruits like bananas and peaches, roots, vegetables, tomatoes, and water plants including waterlily bulbs. Many years ago, Mike King, a timber cruiser working in British Columbia, saw a Bigfoot bending over a water hole washing roots, which he then placed in two neat piles. He ran off up the hillside when he realized he was being watched.[43]

In the second half of the twentieth century the range of Bigfoot's diet has broadened with the inclusion of humans' food, obtained from garbage cans or, occasionally, from people who like being visited and leave out food. Bigfoot has developed a taste for such things as pastry, cooked chicken, and sandwiches, though one did leave behind a peanut butter and jelly (jam) sandwich, left out for it among other table scraps in New Jersey in 1966.[44]

This brief survey of Bigfoot's behaviour has of necessity had to omit many interesting reports. Bigfoot has been seen performing a number of likely and unlikely actions, such as tearing open bags of salt, ripping open an electric power box, jumping on a car roof, throwing dirt through a car window, tossing a tyre and rim, smashing 20 feet (6 metres) of sluiceway into pieces against a tree, throwing a goose at a woman, throwing rocks, playing with a camp fire, destroying camping equipment, chasing people but not attempting to catch them, clam-digging on the beach, spiking fish on sticks. Also, if the reports are accurate, Bigfoot's behaviour can take even stranger forms, like disappearing in a flash of light, and it is these weird reports which we shall discuss in the next chapter.

FIVE: NON-PHYSICAL BIGFOOT AND THE UFO LINK

In most encounters with Bigfoot the witnesses see nothing which might lead them to think that what they are witnessing is anything other than 100 per cent physical. However, this is not always so, and some reports contain features which can only be called weird.

The feature that crops up most frequently is Bigfoot's supposed invulnerability to gunfire. There are a surprising number of cases in which a Bigfoot has been shot at, but has appeared to be unaffected. One such case we have already described in Chapter 1, which involved Charles Fulton of Maysville, Kentucky, who in October 1980 shot at a white-haired Bigfoot which he saw outside his home. Two shots with a 22-calibre pistol seemed to have no effect.[1] Of course we cannot be sure how good the witness's aim was in a case like this, and there are several questions we need to ask: How good a marksman was he under normal circumstances? Was he wearing his glasses? How close was the Bigfoot? Was it a moving target? Could he see it clearly in the darkness/mist/foliage? Even if all the answers are favourable, there remains the element of fear to spoil the aim of even the keenest shot.

Sometimes the witness is sure that he did not miss. A Bigfoot that kept coming to the Sites farm at Wantage, New Jersey, in May 1977, was cornered in the farmyard by Mr Sites and friends. They opened fire on it, using a .222 magnum rifle and a .410 shotgun, and it ran into a shed and out again through a window. Seeing it standing under a tree with its arms outstretched, Mr Sites 'shot at it three or four times with deer slugs in my .410 gauge shotgun, and I know I hit it.' But the Bigfoot simply growled at them, and the men retreated to the house to reload. Mr Sites later chased the Bigfoot in his truck, but it escaped.[2]

Tim Meissner, who saw a Bigfoot near Dunn Lake in British Columbia in April 1979, shot at the creature from 50 feet (15 metres): 'I was aiming for right between his eyes and he went down on one knee and one hand. At first I thought he was dead, but I guess I only grazed him, because he got up and ran away at about 30 miles [48 kilometres] an hour.'[3] Some witnesses have fired into a Bigfoot from very close range, but with no apparent effect. It is possible that the creature's bulk (Tim Meissner's Bigfoot was 9 feet [2.7 metres] tall, as measured against a tree) is such that the guns used are not powerful enough to do any immediately noticeable damage. The Bigfoot can run away apparently unaffected, but if the bullet has entered the body, its effects are likely to cause the creature considerable pain over a long period of time.

That Bigfeet *are* injured by gunfire is suggested by a number of reports. In September 1981 fourteen-year-old Robert Hunt saw a tall, dark creature while walking near his home at Swainsville, North Carolina. He saw it from a distance of 50 feet (15 metres), ran home and grabbed a shotgun. He went out and shot at the creature, which seemed to have been hit. His mother glimpsed it and said, 'It was dragging one leg like it was hurt.'[4] However, there is no indication from the press report whether or not this Bigfoot was dragging its leg before being fired at, or whether the limp did seem to be a definite result of the boy's action, though the report does seem to suggest the latter. On balance it seems likely that Bigfoot is not invulnerable to gunfire at all, but just appears to be invulnerable because the guns used are not big enough for the job. Only a shot between the eyes from close range with a powerful weapon such as those used by big-game hunters could test Bigfoot's supposed invulnerability.

Insubstantiality and other non-physical aspects

Some of the other weird aspects of Bigfoot reports involve insubstantiality. A creature seen at Roachdale, Indiana, in 1972 left no tracks even in mud, and one witness thought she could see through it.[5] This Bigfoot was also silent when passing through foliage. Near Kinderhook, New York, in February 1981, huge footprints in snow began in the middle of a field.[6] At Sykesville, Maryland, in 1973, Bigfeet reportedly disappeared when shot at close range, the same being reported from Uniontown, Pennsylvania, in 1974, where a woman shot at a tall, hairy, apelike creature at her front door, using a 16-gauge shotgun kept by the door to frighten dogs away. As the creature raised its arms above its head, the woman pointed the gun at its midriff and fired, whereupon the creature disappeared in a flash of light.[7]

Other weird reports describe a Bigfoot changing its shape; creatures carrying glowing spheres; an attraction to aluminium trailers and women; a witness possessed by a Bigfoot, and then acting and sounding like one; disembodied voices; a sticky green substance found where a greenish creature with green eyes was seen; and so on. This list could easily be a page longer, but individually the cases do not carry much weight because each weird feature is only supported by one report. Because of possible witness fallibility, several reports from independent witnesses of each type of weird feature would be needed before such reports could be given much credence. So although they are intriguing, they do not constitute much in the way of evidence for a non-physical aspect to Bigfoot. Also, when the total number of such reports is compared with the number of Bigfoot sightings on record, which now numbers over 2,000, it is clear that the percentage of reports showing weird features is extremely small, and that such reports are not representative of the Bigfoot phenomenon as a whole. Their contribution to the Bigfoot mystery will be assessed in our final chapter.

The UFO connection

Some of the weird reports also possess another feature which we have not yet considered – the presence of UFOs. The term 'UFO' is used to describe all types of phenomena from indeterminate lights in the sky, usually seen at night, to massive structured craft, seen at close quarters in the sky or on the ground, by day or night. In the majority of cases, the UFOs seen by Bigfoot witnesses are lights rather than craft, as the following data will show. UFOs were reported in Pennsylvania and at Sykesville, Maryland, in 1973 in the areas where apparently non-physical Bigfeet were seen, and the Roachdale Bigfoot of 1972 is said to have appeared only hours after a mysterious glowing object had exploded silently over a field.[8]

More recently, Bigfoot sightings in western Pennsylvania have apparently involved both non-physical features and UFOs. In the spring of 1979, Sam and Ruth Frew saw a large object tumbling from the sky, and two weeks afterwards started hearing a strange noise, which Mrs Frew described as follows: 'The sound is not a bark, squeal, squawk, or howling sound. In fact we don't know how to describe it. It travels quite fast. It seems like it's on one hillside one second, the next second it's on another hill. Once anyone hears it they never forget it. It makes your skin want to crawl.' Over the next three years, 'Mystery', as the family christened the strange events, revealed itself in various ways: strange smells, three-toed footprints, a continuation of the strange noises which made farm animals nervous, mystery lights which caused bad headaches. On 12 August 1981 Sam Frew saw a 12-foot (3.6 metres) hairy creature in the woods after receiving a mental message to 'Come back down to the gas line', which was where he saw the creature. Next day he found three-toed footprints there. In July 1981, two neighbours had seen a black panther while they were driving on a country back road. They stopped very close to it and as it stood there for ten minutes they noted its 4-foot (1.2 metres) long body, equally long tail, sleek fur, small head, small pointed ears, and long legs. Finally the animal walked slowly out of sight. Later in the summer other sightings of the black cat were reported, as were sightings of mystery lights, and of Bigfoot. Sam Frew felt that the creature had tried to communicate with him by telepathy. He said: 'They are intelligent. It tries to communicate. It is not from this dimension; this is why you only find a few footprints and they disappear.'9 An investigator later decided that some of the lights, those which lit up the trees in the orchard, were coming from vehicles travelling along a road over half a mile away, but although the Frews agreed that this could be an explanation for some of the lights, they still felt that other lights they had observed could not have been caused in this way.10

The Frew case is a typical example of an apparent connection between UFOs and Bigfoot phenomena (with another strange animal, the black panther, turning up just to complicate things). There are two types of cases showing this apparent connection. In the first category, the UFO and Bigfoot sightings take place at the same time and in the same area, and are usually seen by the same witness. In the second category, UFO and Bigfoot sightings are reported from the same area over a period of time, say several weeks or a couple of months.

Those reports which would definitely establish a link between UFOs and Bigfoot, where a UFO in the form of a solid craft is seen on the ground or very close, with a Bigfoot seen inside the craft or close to it if outside, are extremely rare. Reports in both categories are not exactly common, in any case. Mark Moravec has collected together as many reports as he could find and published his data as *The UFO-Anthropoid Catalogue*.[11] He found fifteen cases in our first category, and forty-eight in the second. But of his fifteen 'close-connection' cases, we consider five to be unreliable in some way – from a dubious source like the sensationalist press, or not involving a creature with enough Bigfoot-type features. When the reports are carefully studied, there are not many that specifically include enough details to enable a clear Bigfoot identification, a major omission often being any mention of a hair-covered body. Admittedly the viewing conditions may not always be suitable for a frightened witness to establish that the giant shape lurking in the bushes is covered with hair! (See the Presque Isle report, detailed shortly, as a good example of this failing.) If we allow ten of Moravec's cases, plus two others post-dating his cut-off date, that makes a total of twelve cases in which a Bigfoot and UFO were seen at the same time and place.

Moravec lists forty-eight cases in category two, still not a large number, even though the conditions have been relaxed to admit cases where the Bigfoot/UFO connection is more tenuous. Even if we increase these numbers to allow for cases that neither we nor Moravec have heard about, and suppose that there are around a hundred cases altogether claiming a UFO/Bigfoot link, that is still only a hundred cases out of the 2,000-plus sightings of Bigfoot on record. Or in percentage terms, roughly 5 per cent of reports include features mildly suggestive of a Bigfoot/UFO link, while only 0.6 per cent show a clear Bigfoot/UFO link.

How good is the evidence for such a Bigfoot/UFO link? Some cases stand up to scrutiny better than others, so let us consider some typical examples, with first of all the eight very best 'category one' cases – UFOs and Bigfeet seen at the same time in the same area by the same witness.

During the summer of 1966 there was a UFO flap

(many sighting reports within a short time) in the Edinboro/ Erie area of Pennsylvania, and a tall 'person or thing' was seen several times on the shore of Edinboro Lake.[12] A similar encounter took place on 31 July at Presque Isle Peninsula Park north of Erie, where four people and two children had gone for a picnic. Their car got stuck in the sand, and while three of the adults waited with the children to be rescued, they saw some strange events. Shortly after 10 p.m. they saw a light land near the beach not far away from them. One of the witnesses, sixteen-year-old Betty Jean Klem, saw it as a mushroom-shaped object with three lights. She said: 'The ship was big. It came half way up between those trees, and when it came down and landed the car vibrated . . . Rays of light shone from the object. It lit up the whole woods along its path. It wasn't like a searchlight. There was light along the ground, along its whole path. When the police car came up to the stuck vehicle, the UFO lights went out.'

The police patrolmen went towards the UFO with Douglas J. Tibbetts, one of the car's occupants, but they had only gone about 300 yards (270 metres) when they heard the car horn blaring. They found Betty Jean Klem and Anita Haifley, with the two young children, in a state of terror. Miss Klem said she had seen 'a dark, apparently featureless creature, not human, maybe animal, which moved sluggishly back into the bush'. She saw it for 1½-2 minutes and noted it was about 6 feet (1.8 metres) tall with no apparent neck or arms. They may have been hanging straight down by its sides, and therefore not noticeable in the gloom, and the poor light at 10.30 p.m. may also account for her not seeing the creature's facial features. Mrs Haifley also saw the creature, and they had both heard scratching noises on the car roof before they saw it. The police took them all for questioning, and police chief Dan Dascanio said: 'I'm convinced that the young people saw something. The girl was a credible person. Of the two individuals involved she was the most specific about what she saw – she made no attempt to fill in her story when she wasn't sure. She was one scared girl when I first saw her. Her hands were shaking, her face was trembling, her speech was more inarticulate, and she had difficulty maintaining her composure. Her eyes were red and she kept shaking her head from side to side.'

Next day two patrolmen returned to the site in the daylight and found markings in the sand where the supposed UFO had landed. They also found marks possibly left by the creature the two women saw. These tracks led from the landing site to within 2 feet (0.6 metres) of where the car was stuck. They were conical in shape, sharply made, and about 9 inches (23 centimetres) in diameter and 6 inches (15 centimetres) deep. They also had marks that looked like claw marks. The tracks were staggered as if their maker had been walking, and were 5-6 feet (1.5-1.8 metres) apart. Later in the day the men found similar prints leading to a lake. Also found was an unidentified clear liquid substance which had not seeped away into the sand as water would. Although no traces of radioactivity were found, the patrolman who collected the samples became ill suddenly about nine hours later, the illness lasting for about three hours. Also noted at the site was a large, freshly gouged area of wood and bark on a willow tree close to the picnic table. And a final physical confirmation that something really did happen that evening: the car was found to have a dent on the roof which was not there when the car was polished only hours before the evening's events.[13] Did the two women really see a Bigfoot-type creature which arrived on the scene in a UFO? Although unfortunately not seen too clearly, the creature certainly resembled a Bigfoot in certain features: its height, absence of a neck, dark colouring, and its behaviour in approaching the car.

1973 was a good year for UFO/Bigfoot reports, but the most amazing of them all was tantalizingly brief, and reached the Westmoreland County UFO Control Center in the form of an anonymous telephone call. The caller described how three women driving through woods near Penn, Pennsylvania, saw a landed UFO, large, metallic and rectangular. They saw a door open, a ramp come down, and three 7-foot (2 metres) hairy apelike creatures ran out and into the woods.[14] This sighting was reported in September 1973, and in October three 'category one' UFO/Bigfoot sightings occurred. The first, early in the month, was at Galveston in Indiana. A man fishing at a lake turned on hearing a noise, thinking it was his companions returning; 20 feet (6 metres) away through the dusk he thought he could see an apelike creature apparently watching him. Although initially frightened, especially when it did not respond to his call, he then became less frightened, for some reason, and was almost upset when the creature left. Minutes later something touched his shoulder, and spinning round he saw a sandy-coloured creature racing away in leaps, 'like a man on a rope being pulled too fast by a car'. He ran after it, and heard its feet slapping as it crossed a hard road. It leapt a ditch and was lost in the woods. Very soon afterwards, the witness saw a glowing bronze object shoot up from the trees into the sky. On returning to the site the next day, the witness saw nothing, but the next evening when accompanied by his fiancée, her father and two friends, they saw a white light in the sky, and a 8-9 foot (2.4-2.7 metres) creature which stood motionless in the tall growth. Even throwing rocks at it did not move it, and they could not recall whether the rocks missed, bounced off or passed right through it. They had to leave to move their vehicle out of the way of another, and when they returned the creature had gone.[15]

Later in the month, on 21 October, a woman awoke at 2.30 a.m. at her home in west Cincinnati, Ohio, and saw lights at ground level. Inside one of them, which was shaped like a 7-foot (2 metres) bell jar, she saw a grey, apelike creature with no neck and a head with a snout. Its arms were moving stiffly up and down alternately. While she was calling the police, everything vanished.[16]

In December 1974 a similar event befell sixty-nine-year-old dairy farmer William Bosak, who was driving home at night through patchy fog in the Frederic area of Wisconsin. He saw a disc-shaped UFO, with a glass front containing a weird figure which stood there with its arms raised. It was brightly lit, and looked scared. Bosak could only see it from the waist up, and it looked human in shape, but its body was covered with dark-tan fur, though the face and chin were bare. The ears stretched out straight from the head for about 3 inches (7 centimetres), while the mouth and nose seemed flat. The witness decided not to stop for a closer look, but drove straight past the object, which was lost to view in the fog.[17]

Only a few days after the Cincinnati sighting, a dramatic encounter took place on a farm near Greensburg, Pennsylvania. At 9 p.m. on 25 October 1973, about fifteen people saw a bright red ball hovering over a field, and one man, whom we shall call Stephen, decided to investigate. He took a rifle, and was accompanied by ten-year-old twin boys. They saw the UFO, about 100 feet (30 metres) in diameter, land in the field: 'It was dome-shaped, just like a big bubble. It was making a sound like a lawn mower.' One of the boys noticed two figures walking by a fence, and Stephen fired over their heads, thinking they were bears. But when they came closer, they seemed to be 7 and 8 feet (2.0 and 2.4 metres) tall, with long dark-greyish hair, long arms and greenish-yellow eyes. They were making a whining noise, as if talking to each other. Afraid of the situation, as the two creatures steadily came closer, Stephen fired over their heads again, and then directly at the larger one. It raised its hand, whining, and both creatures turned slowly and moved back towards the woods. The UFO had disappeared leaving a bright glowing area. Stephen immediately reported the events to the police, and a trooper came out.

When he and Stephen went to the field, they could see the glowing ring, and heard a walking noise in the woods, with the sound of trees being broken. Stephen thought he saw a figure, and fired at it. After half an hour at the site, both men were on edge, and Stephen was very excitable. The trooper decided to alert Stan Gordon and his colleagues from Westmoreland County UFO Study Group, and they arrived at 1.30 a.m. While being questioned at the site, Stephen began to behave strangely, growling and waving his arms, before finally collapsing. Some of the other men felt ill, and they all decided it would be best to leave.[18]

Occasionally UFO/Bigfoot cases are reported from other countries, and Mark Moravec has recorded in his catalogue several from such places as Australia, Spain and Argentina. A 'category one' report appeared in the Argentinian press in November 1979, a tantalizingly vague report of a judge and an architect seeing, 'a short time ago', a 'spaceship manned by an extraterrestrial who looked like a hairy gorilla'. The men were on Punta de Damas hill near Santiago in Chile when they saw a round object with bright coloured lights. Beside it stood 'a strange individual of humanoid features, with a strange head attached to the body without a neck, completely covered with hairs'. As they began to approach, the UFO took off vertically at high speed.[19]

The most recent UFO/Bigfoot report known to us comes from the Rome area of Ohio, where in the summer of 1981 the occupants of a rural property were seeing tall, red-eyed hairy creatures close to the house and in the woods. In one encounter on 25 June, a creature was shot at with a 4-10 shotgun, right between the eyes, but it ran off before a second shot could be fired. On the following night the same witness again saw the creature and claims to have hit it with his flashlight. It had stood by a hoist, and so afterwards its height could be assessed as about 9½ feet (2.9 metres). Its long shaggy hair was black or dark brown. It had a big flat nose, and big eyes which glowed red. Many more sightings followed, but all attempts to shoot and poison the creatures failed. The investigators, who saw the creatures themselves, found circular footprints 7 inches (17 centimetres) wide and 8 inches (20 centimetres) long, with 'three toe-like extensions'. Five-toed prints were also found. During the events, the woods would light up 'as bright as day' for no apparent reason. Glowing spheres of light were seen, and once when an object flew overhead, one witness shot at it, hearing the bullet hit something that sounded like glass.[20]

The eight cases just described constitute the very best evidence available to support the idea that there is a UFO/Bigfoot link. The rest of the cases, those in 'category two', are suggestive of a link, though as the UFO and Bigfoot events did not take place side by side, their occurrence in the same area could be considered co-incidental. A few cases of this type follow.

On 18 May 1969 the residents of a rural area near Rising Sun, Indiana, suffered a power blackout. During the previous weeks mystery lights had been seen along a nearby ridge. On 19 May, George Kaiser saw a strange figure in his farmyard.

I watched it for about two minutes before it saw me. It stood in a fairly upright position although it was bent over about in the middle of its back, with arms about the same height as a normal human being. I'd say it was about five-eight [1.7 metres] or so and it had a very muscular structure. The head sat directly on the shoulder and the face was black, with hair that stuck out on the back of its head; it had eyes set close together and a very short forehead. It was covered with hair except for the back of the hands and the face. The hands looked like normal hands, not claws.

It finally ran off at speed, leaving four-toed tracks. On the following evening a neighbour watched for eight minutes as a glowing, greenish-white object moved about in the sky overhead.[21]

In Puerto Rico in 1975 there was a spate of mysterious animal deaths and UFO sightings, and while these events were continuing a hospital janitor, Orlando Franceschi, had a night-time encounter with a 'horrible monster' at his home in Ponce. Looking out of the window, he saw what he thought at first was a dog passing by, but when he realized that his own dog was tied up outside, he grabbed a shovel and went outside. He saw the creature close by, and noticed its long ears, long nose, slitlike mouth with no lips, eyes like two black blobs, and an apelike jawbone. It was less than 5 feet (1.5 metres) tall and swayed as it walked. Franceschi hit it three times with his shovel before he fell to the ground, paralysed. When he was able to get up again, the creature had gone away through a gap in the fence.[22] Unfortunately, this report is not sufficiently detailed for us to judge if this really was a Bigfoot-type creature, since Franceschi does not mention if it was clothed or hair-covered. But his mention of an ape's jawbone does suggest that the creature seemed somehow apelike to him.

Although this chapter's sightings have mostly been located away from the traditional Bigfoot territory in the north-west, this area is not completely free of UFO sightings. But as there are so many Bigfoot reports from the area, it is much more likely that any UFOs sighted close in time and space to Bigfoot sightings can be ascribed purely to chance. For example, around 1979-80 an English lady, Mrs Cross, who lived at the small village of Patricia Bay on Canada's Vancouver Island, described how she and four neighbours watched a large white light come in from the north and hover over the sea for ten minutes before flying off to the north again. This happened on two successive nights. The morning after the second sighting, an Indian living on the nearby reservation was woken by dogs barking furiously around 5 a.m. and he saw an enormous 'gorilla' climbing out of the sea. It climbed up the bank, through the trees, and ran off incredibly fast down the road.[23] The fact that it was an Indian who saw the creature makes a tidy link between the present-day UFO/Bigfoot reports and Indian lore on this subject. The Gabrielino Indians of southern California believed in the existence of Towis or Takwis, a giant hairy cannibal, who was also associated with bright flashes of light and flying luminescent balls. This lore dates back 200 years.[24] In the 1880s an Indian led a man to a cave in Tennessee where a hairy manlike creature was living, with food provided regularly by the Indians. They believed that this creature and others like it came from 'moons' which landed from time to time in the valley.[25]

In trying to assess the nature of the UFO/Bigfoot link, it is clear to us that in some ways the Bigfeet seen in connection with UFOs differ from those reported earlier in this book and having no known UFO connections. As already pointed out, not many of the Bigfeet with a close UFO link have been seen well enough or described minutely enough for us to be absolutely certain that the creatures were really Bigfeet, but clearly they do show striking similarities. Noticeable differences are the three-toed footprints (or in the case of Presque Isle, cone-shaped prints), which are not usually reported in non-UFO Bigfoot sightings; and the fact that many of the UFO-linked Bigfeet have red glowing eyes, at least that is the experience of Stan Gordon from his Pennsylvania investigation and research.[26] Although glowing eyes, sometimes red, have been reported in non-UFO cases, this feature does seem more frequent in UFO-related cases.

The most striking difference between UFO and non-UFO cases is their location. While the large majority of the non-UFO Bigfoot sightings are reported from the north-west USA and western Canada, the majority of UFO-related sightings are reported from the central and eastern USA. We did a rough analysis of the locations mentioned in Mark Moravec's catalogue and found that Pennsylvania had the highest number of reports, with the adjoining states of Ohio and Indiana next on the list. Other eastern and central states mentioned, though with only one or two cases each, were Wisconsin, Michigan, New York, Massachusetts, New Jersey, West Virginia, Florida, Illinois, Missouri. Further west, South Dakota, Montana and Colorado had a few cases, while California was the only true western state which had several reports. It is quite clear that the non-UFO Bigfoot is a creature mainly of the north-west (though also being seen in central and eastern USA), while the UFO-Bigfoot definitely prefers the eastern states. Why this should be is not clear, but it may have something to do with the media climate in the east, or simply with the fact that the principal supporters and investigators of weird cases live in the central and eastern states. Our next and final chapter, discussing the theories offered to explain the nature of the world's hairy man-beasts, may provide more answers.

SIX:
SEARCHING FOR ANSWERS

Do man-beasts really exist? Those people who have heard in passing of the Yeti or Bigfoot automatically doubt their reality, because they have been brought up to believe that man has his finger on the pulse of the planet and knows virtually everything there is to know about it. That is not true, and the evidence for the existence of man-beasts that we have presented in this book represents only a small part of the evidence available. The doubter will also claim that misidentifications or hoaxes can account for the reports, but the former is unlikely in view of all the close sightings and convincing footprints. Hoaxers do occasionally muddy the waters, especially with faked footprints, but are largely irrelevant to the overall picture, despite the media attention they sometimes get. In 1982 eighty-six-year-old Rant Mullens of Toledo, Washington, claimed that he had been hoaxing footprints for half a century, by means of fake feet he carved from wood. He also claimed responsibility for the 1924 Ape Canyon affair, when a group of miners said that their cabin was bombarded with rocks thrown by giant hairy creatures. Mullens' version was that

My uncle, George Ross, and I were fishing in the area (now known as Ape Canyon) in 1924. As we hiked out, we heard some miners talking at the bottom of the canyon. They had fashioned a ladder out of poles to get down the steep cliff.

George was always playing jokes, so he and I rolled some rocks down over the edge. Then we got out of there fast. When we heard that the miners were telling hairy ape stories, we both had a good laugh. We never told anyone the true story.[1]

This version does not agree with the story as told by Fred Beck, one of the miners, who said that they saw the man-beasts and shot at them, and that their cabin was bombarded. It is impossible to be sure whether Beck and Mullens were talking about the same incident.

We have already emphasized how difficult it is to fake realistic footprints that will fool the expert (see Chapter 4). In 1978 or 1979 a pair of boots was found near the White River in Stone County, Arkansas. They had pieces of tyre cut in the shape of large feet fastened to their soles.[2] Although prints made by this method might fool some people, closer examination by someone with experience of Bigfoot tracks would soon reveal them as faked. The depth is one giveaway. After Scott and Neal Brown had found large footprints near a house in Skamania County, Washington, on 1 December 1982, they made a wooden foot and both stood on it, a total weight of 405 pounds (183 kilograms). It sank half an inch (12 millimetres) into the ground, as compared with the one and three-eighths inches (35 millimetres) of the genuine prints.[3]

Hoaxes are clearly not the answer to the man-beast mystery. But, say the sceptics, if Bigfoot really exists, where are the corpses or bones? Why, in all these confrontations between armed men and Bigfeet, are no Bigfeet ever killed? As we have already suggested, the guns used may simply not be powerful enough. But over the years a number of reports of man-beasts being killed or captured have emerged. Unfortunately, no corpses exist to support these claims, except for 'Bozo', and he is elusive. The two reports which follow illustrate the problems.

In December 1967 two students out shooting in Teton

Forest, Wyoming, killed what they at first thought was a bear. When they looked closely at the body, they found it was humanlike, about 7 feet (2 metres) tall, and covered in dark brown hair except for the palms and soles of the feet. Its eyeteeth were longer than the other teeth. (Fangs are sometimes reported by Bigfoot witnesses.) Wondering what they had killed, and thinking it must belong to someone, they decided to leave the corpse where it was and keep quiet about the affair.[4] In August 1969, some people camping near Auburn, Washington, heard a disturbance in the bush, but were too scared to leave their tents during darkness. Next morning they found a bear trap containing a 20-inch (50 centimetres) hair-covered foot. Huge footprints led from the trap, with patches of blood taking the place of one foot's print. They left the foot where it was.[5] In both these cases, if the reports are true, the witnesses did not know about Bigfoot, else they would surely have realized the enormous value of what they had seen. Both parties' decisions not to report their strange finds verge on the unbelievable, and perhaps both reports are tall tales.

It is not really strange that no one has ever stumbled upon the bones of a Bigfoot that has died a natural death, or even an unnatural one. It is possible that they may even conceal or bury their dead; but it is more likely that nature disposes of the remains. Apart from Bigfoot, bones of all other wild animals are rarely found, either.

So far, those people devoted to the task of obtaining public and scientific recognition for Bigfoot and other man-beasts have not been particularly successful. Without solid physical proof, flesh or bones rather than footprints and photographs, the scientists have been unwilling to jeopardize their professional reputations by being seen to chase phantoms. They are aware, perhaps without exactly realizing it, of the attitude towards such phenomena that is common among those who are ignorant of the true facts. The unknown breeds fear, and fear breeds a defensive attitude of ridicule. This results in harassment of witnesses, especially children. Thirteen-year-old Tina Barone, who may have touched a Bigfoot, was ridiculed by her schoolmates: 'They tell me I'm stupid and didn't see anything.'[6] Despite this problem, some scientists have courageously taken an active part in Bigfoot research, for example Professor Grover Krantz whose work on footprints we described in Chapter 4. In the 1980s there has been a growing acceptance in the scientific community that there is something in the forests that needs investigation. However, Professor Krantz has repeatedly pointed out that the scientists must have flesh or bones as solid proof of the existence of Bigfoot. 'I tell you quite bluntly I'm out to prove that Sasquatch exists and the only way to do that is to bring back a piece of the body.' He himself carries a 'Sasquatch cannon' – a .358-calibre Magnum rifle that can kill a mature grizzly bear. A hunter who manages to kill a Bigfoot but cannot transport the body back to civilization should cut off the biggest piece he can carry, say the head or lower jaw, plus a hand or foot. At the very least bring the fourth tooth on the side of the jaw, which will tell the anthropologists what has been killed, says Krantz.[7]

Hunters anxious to be the first to bring back a Bigfoot, and probably earn themselves fame and fortune as a result, are often reported in the media as they prepare for their next expedition, but this is always followed by silence. In the press during May 1981 C. Thomas Biscardi claimed to have seen and photographed a Bigfoot during April while tracking it on Mount Lassen in northern California, and he was planning to capture one alive by dropping a smoke bomb from a helicopter 'to put it to sleep'. This was to take place in Arizona's Superstition Mountains, but we have heard no news of his success.[8] In 1982 Ernest Sproles, founder of Sportsmen for Christ, Incorporated, was planning to kill a Bigfoot in order to make the scientists take it seriously. For the 'Christian

Bigfoot Project' he planned to budget expenses of $100,000, and to use a 458 Winchester as sometimes used on African safaris. When told that he would probably be arrested for killing a non-game animal in California, he commented: 'Unless God gives me a turnaround with the Fish and Game Department, I'll have to kill some Bigfoot in another state.'[9] Such expeditions as these are unlikely to happen anywhere other than in the mind of the 'hunter', and it is probable that lack of resources is what prevents genuine $100,000 expeditions from making a serious attempt to bring back a Bigfoot corpse.

Not everyone believes that a Bigfoot should be shot. Some witnesses, gun aimed and ready to fire, could not pull the trigger because the creature looked somehow human. We are not sure yet whether the creature is human or animal, and the paradox is that we are unlikely to know for sure until the scientists can examine a corpse. If it turns out to be human, murder will have been committed, but no doubt some scientists will consider this justified for the advancement of scientific knowledge. Dmitri Bayanov of Moscow's Darwin Museum argues that rather than the Bigfoot being taken to the scientists, the scientists should go to the Bigfoot, that is that they should go and study man-beasts in their natural habitat, in the same way that Jane Goodall and George Schaller have studied higher primates in the wild. Jane Goodall confirmed Bayanov's feelings in a letter to him, concluding: 'to shoot a creature just to see what it is – well, that is even worse. Most undesirable ethically – and the mark of a poor researcher.'[10] But a field study of Bigfoot would present many problems, even if it could be afforded, not least being the fact that Bigfoot is a secretive loner, and before study could begin the scientists would have to discover some method of getting Bigfoot to come out into the open, and making friends with him.

Prehistoric survivals?

In the absence of physical evidence that can be analysed in order to ascertain what Bigfoot really is, theories have proliferated. It does seem likely that more than one explanation will be needed to encompass the variations in the reports worldwide. The most popular idea is that man-beasts are surviving prehistoric men, and it seems very likely that in some cases this is the answer. We have already referred to Neanderthal Man in the USSR (Chapter 2) and Australopithecus in Africa (Chapter 3), and there seems every possibility that most of the other man-beasts living in remote corners of the world could also be relict hominids. In the battle for supremacy between different kinds of men, those that lost may not just have been exterminated or died out, but may have retreated to the wilderness areas, where they have lived unmolested to the present day. As human incursion into their habitat increases, sightings become more frequent – and the creature's future is threatened. Russian researcher Professor Boris Porshnev and French researcher Dr Bernard Heuvelmans were the first to announce that Neanderthal man still survives in the USSR,[11] while more recently Myra Shackley has confirmed their opinion in her book *Wildmen*.

Determining the identity of each type of man-beast would be a complex and uncertain undertaking. Ivan Sanderson concluded that the types differed according to the vegetational type of the place where they lived. and he divided the man-beasts into four main categories, beginning with those most like humans and ending with the least manlike: 1. *Sub-humans* (East Eurasia and Oriental), e.g. Malayan and Yunnan creatures, and Ksy-Giiks and Almas, both possibly Neanderthal. 2. *Proto-pygmies* (Orient, Africa, possibly central and north-west South America), e.g. Dwendis, Shiru, Sedapas, Sehites, Agogwes, Tel-Imas. 3. *Neo-giants* (Indo-China, East Eurasia, North and South America), e.g. Dzu-Teh, Sasquatch/Bigfoot, Mapinguary and Didi. 4. *Sub-hominids* (south-central Eurasia including Himalayas), e.g. Meh-Teh.[12] Sanderson makes no mention of the Australian man-beast, which was probably not known to him when he was working on his book *Abominable Snowmen: Legend Come to Life* over twenty years ago. His first two categories are probably relict hominids, his neo-giants may be Gigantopithecus, and his sub-hominids may be 'an early offshoot of the Pongids [apes]'.[13]

Gigantopithecus

Sanderson's suggestion that the Bigfoot and similar creatures could be a form of Gigantopithecus (though he was not necessarily the first to make this suggestion – we are not sure who was) has found favour with other researchers. Sanderson calls Gigantopithecus 'an enormous something', which sums up the lack of real information on this creature which used to live in southern China some 500,000 years ago. There is not even agreement about whether it was an ape or a human! Sanderson decided, having examined a tooth, that it was a hominid. Dr Bernard Heuvelmans would not commit himself in his book *On the Track of Unknown Animals*, settling for 'giant ape man'.[14] Grover Krantz justifies his instructions to hunters to kill a Bigfoot by emphasizing that it is an animal, and not even semi-human. He also accepts that Bigfoot might possibly be a Gigantopithecus, so presumably he believes that Gigantopithecus is not human.[15]

Gigantopithecus has only been known about since 1937, when Dr von Koenigswald found a huge tooth among fossil bones and teeth in a Chinese apothecary's store in Hong Kong.[16] Now a total of four lower jaws and over a thousand teeth have come to light, and Chinese anthropology professor Wu Rukang has made a study based on comparative anatomy in order to try and determine what Gigantopithecus might have looked like. The result surprisingly close to the 'wild men' reported in China. Professor Wu also said that Gigantopithecus was omnivorous, and would have walked on two legs. Classification was difficult, since it was man and yet not man, ape and yet not ape: 'To classify the Gigantopithecus as belonging to the predecessors of man and not yet the real man is more appropriate,' Professor Wu concluded.[17] Those who criticize some Bigfoot researchers for romantically seeing Bigfoot as a missing link between apes and humans should withhold their judgement for a while longer. In the absence of any more appropriate contender, we will tentatively identify Bigfoot as Gigantopithecus, and await developments in research into both the Gigantopithecus of 500,000 years ago, and the Bigfoot of today. It seems likely that Gigantopithecus originated in China and gradually spread around the world via land-bridges, settling in the vast forests of North and South America, and probably in Australia too. There he would have continued to live happily; but in the twentieth century man's greed resulted in rapid deforestation, which makes it ever more difficult for Gigantopithecus to maintain successful breeding populations. He may at last be nearing extinction.

Dr John Napier wrote of *four* candidates 'as progenitors of Bigfoot',[18] including as well as Gigantopithecus and Neanderthal Man two others less often mentioned: Paranthropus robustus and Java Man (Homo erectus). Paranthropus lived in Africa for 3-5 million years, and seems to have been a bipedal (though clumsy) walker, vegetarian, and like Gigantopithecus apparently neither ape nor man, though Dr Napier states that he was 'unquestionably more man-like than *Gigantopithecus*.'[19] Java Man was much more advanced, in fact probably too advanced to be recognizable as Bigfoot, for he used fire, was a hunter, and made tools. Dr Napier conceded that Neanderthal Man may be responsible for Almas reports, and leaned towards either Gigantopithecus or Paranthropus as a possible Bigfoot identification, but even with all his knowledge it is clear that he was loth to make a definitive statement on the matter. In *Bigfoot* he concluded

Dr John Napier.

his chapter on fossil evidence:

Gigantopithecus is generally regarded as an aberrant ape, while *Paranthropus* is conceded to be, by some authorities at least, an aberrant human. It would be a neat solution to allocate the ape-like *Gigantopithecus* to the Himalayas and the more human-like *Paranthropus* to North America, but it would be a shockingly unscientific thing to do.

Although the idea of Neanderthal and Gigantopithecus survival was first published many years ago, few people apart from the hardcore of man-beast researchers have taken it seriously. At first glance it seems impossible that prehistoric survivals could be sharing the planet without man knowing of it. But this is the attitude of egocentric man, rather than realistic man. We occupy only a small proportion of the earth's surface, and the rest is left unvisited and unknown. Ivan Sanderson pointed out that in 1960 a large herd of the Woodland Bison was unexpectedly discovered in the Canadian Northwest Territories, and in 1938 the Kouprey, the second biggest member of the ox family, turned up in Indo-China, having been unknown until then but now actually quite common.[20] When the Kouprey was first reported, scientists called the reports lies. There are strong possibilities that prehistoric survivals await discovery in many lakes of the world, not to mention the oceans; scientists have recently been chasing dinosaurs in deepest Africa; and there is even a possibility that an as yet unknown species of big cat has lived undiscovered in Britain since the last ice age. Sightings of big cats have been reported regularly throughout England, Scotland and Wales, and recent fieldwork by naturalist Di Francis has produced strong evidence that our island is home to a unique cat.[21] An increase in sightings in recent decades is again due to pressure on the creature's habitat. Without that pressure, all these creatures can easily live unseen by man. That this is feasible is confirmed by anthropology professor Charles A. Reed:

I've never met a Bigfoot, and haven't seen a track even (other than a cast), although I've walked and ridden horseback over much of the country from which they've been reported, but when I was wandering around in the Oregon Cascades as a youth I had never heard of a Bigfoot and so wasn't looking for one. I had heard of wolves (at that time still present in western Oregon) and of pumas, but I never saw those animals either, so not seeing a Bigfoot was not so remarkable. I grew up on a farm in Hood River valley, just north of Mt. Hood, and only 20 miles [32 kilometres] west of The Dalles, where sightings of Bigfoot were reported only a few years ago, but I walked or rode horse (and later drove) over much of that backcountry and only once saw a bear, and they don't particularly try to hide. So, from this background, I understand how even a large animal, if wary and intelligent, could fade into those forests, particularly if the population-density is low.[22]

Explaining pseudo-Bigfeet

No one has suggested yet that Gigantopithecus has the ability to disappear, so how do we explain those reports with the weird features which we outlined in Chapter 5, and also those reports involving UFOs? Although such reports are few in number when compared with the 'conventional' reports, and also sometimes suffer from sensationalized reporting, nevertheless there seems to be a genuine phenomenon causing these 'pseudo-Bigfoot' reports which needs explanation. Here we are on boggy ground, even more uncertain than when we were classifying man-beasts as prehistoric survivals, and all our attempts to explain the pseudo-Bigfoot should be considered as totally speculative.[23]

That the UFOs accompanying the pseudo-Bigfeet usually take the form of lights rather than solid craft may be a clue to the process at work. Light suggests energy, and both UFOs and pseudo-Bigfeet may be nothing more than expressions of energy. The energy could come from several sources. R. Martin Wolf commented on the high incidence of Bigfoot sightings, also UFO appearances, cattle mutilations and paranormal phenomena, close to 'microwave towers, high-tension power lines, nuclear power installations, hydro-electric dams, bodies of water, missile silos, railroad tracks and even mobile homes.' He further pointed out that 'all of these... are affected by the transmission of electromagnetic energy'.[24] Some UFO researchers have recently sought to identify UFOs as 'earth lights', or electro-magnetic manifestations released from the earth as a result of stress deep within the rock,[25] and Dr Michael A. Persinger suggests that the 'rich imagery' sometimes experienced by UFO witnesses at close quarters to the phenomenon, i.e. solid craft and UFO entities, may be the result of 'the direct interference of these electromagnetic fields with the human brain'.[26] We can extend this idea to suggest that some people might see Bigfoot rather than UFO entities.

UFO writer John A. Keel suggested the possibility that UFO entities sometimes materialize by using energy drawn from the witness, a process he called 'kinetic vampirism'.[27] Pseudo-Bigfeet could also utilize such a process. They might normally exist in another dimension and thus be invisible to us, able to emerge into our world only when fuelled by an available energy source, be it human energy, or one of the sources listed by R. Martin Wolf. Perhaps the materializations are involuntary – why would they want or need to become visible to us? Of course, any entity or creature seen through the process suggested by Persinger would have no external reality; they would exist solely within the mind of the witness. If some of this speculation seems rather far-fetched we should emphasize that it is only theoretical, and so far there is no experimental proof for any of it. Nevertheless, pseudo-Bigfeet *are* seen, and sometimes in conjunction with strange lights, and two instances of the UFO/Bigfoot link as reported by reliable witnesses will help to demonstrate the phenomenon at close hand.

In July 1975 Peter Guttilla was camping near Bluff Creek (where Roger Patterson filmed a Bigfoot) in northwest California, following reports of globes of orange or red light and bright flashes of light. He took earthquake sensors with him, hoping by this means to be alerted to the presence of any heavy nocturnal visitors. Around 3 a.m. on the second night he was woken by buzzes, bleeps and flashing lights as his equipment registered 'something'. Outside the tent there was nothing to be seen, though he sensed a 'presence' towards the west. In that direction a small speck of orange and yellow light suddenly rose from the trees. It came towards him and stopped overhead before vanishing straight up. At dawn he found several 17-inch (43 centimetre) footprints near by, though he does not state whether they appeared to have been very recently made.[28]

Across the continent in New York State, Bruce G. Hallenbeck has for several years closely followed the activities of the so-called 'Kinderhook Creature', which has left traces in the form of footprints, headless rabbits, and rabbits stuffed into a snowbank as if being stored for the winter. On the night of 5 May 1982, Hallenbeck went out to the woods hoping to see or at least hear the creatures, as he had done before. He sat in his car for a while, and then, just when he began to think of leaving, he heard a strange noise no more than 30 yards (27 metres) away.

The sound is difficult to describe, but it's unmistakeable. For one thing, you know when 'it's' around, because everything else becomes silent. The crickets stop chirping, the nightbirds stop calling.

The sound was a sort of combination of the kind of squeal a pig makes when it's being slaughtered, and that of a monkey or ape trying to speak. An improbable combination, but that's the closest I can come to describing it. It sounded as though there were two communicating with each other.

Here was my chance at last. My mind wanted to see what it was, but my legs refused to move. It was as though I were paralyzed. When I finally did get up the courage to get out of the car and cross the road to the edge of the field, the noises stopped. But then came the *really* weird part. Immediately after the sounds ceased, a round white light appeared over the field, floated up into the sky and vanished before my eyes. I swear on a stack of Bibles it's true.

He added that he believes one of the creature's favourite areas, Cushing's Hill, has an Indian mound buried under the thick brush, as he has found ancient stone fences and standing stones in the area already, and commented that the creature could somehow be connected with the mound.[29] This is not a totally fanciful idea, in view of the UFO (earth light?) he saw, and the connection made by Paul Devereux between earth lights and prehistoric sites in Britain.[30] Early man may have marked the major sources of earth energy with stones and mounds, for reasons which are not yet clear to us.

*   *   *   *

In the vast jigsaw which is the Bigfoot mystery, the pieces which will allow us to positively identify the creature as Neanderthal Man, or Gigantopithecus, or whatever, are still missing. So, too, are the pieces that would enable us to see clearly the link between UFO, Bigfoot and energy sources; but there are plenty of clues for anyone who wishes to continue the search for the missing pieces. If neither of those puzzles appeals to you, there are still more theories, all of them posing more questions than answers. We believe it is safe to reject the idea that Bigfeet are experimental animals dropped from UFOs by extraterrestrials, or that the man-beasts are themselves extraterrestrials piloting UFOs. More worthy of consideration is D. Scott Rogo's suggestion 'that they are psychic projections just as are UFOs, miracles, and poltergeists. Something from us "projects out", takes on a physical form and a vestige of intelligence, and then disappears as the force which gave it birth dissipates.'[31] Questions arising include, How could these projections occur, and why? Perhaps they occur as a result of the Bigfoot image being 'in the air'. When any phenomenon, be it UFOs, mystery animals, or whatever, is subjected to media attention, one result might be that people manufacture their own sightings – unwittingly, for the vision seems quite real to them. Or the phenomenon might feed on the energy aroused by people's interest in it, and thus be able to achieve apparent solidity. John Michell and Robert Rickard have suggested a variation on this idea, to account for man-beasts worldwide. They speculate that, since the time of Darwin and the beginning of the search for 'ape-men', people began thinking about ape-men and hoping to find conclusive proof of their earlier existence. As a result of the 'frustrated desires of the evolutionists for relics of ape-like human ancestors', the thought-forms have taken on a kind of reality.[32]

Psychologists would prefer to call it 'wishful thinking', and to some extent they may be right. We do need our gods, our monsters, and our mysteries, and when Bigfoot mania is in the air, a shadow becomes a hairy giant, a formless mark in the mud becomes a huge footprint. But are the thousands of witnesses all around the world, both from primitive and technologically advanced societies, all unable to differentiate between myths and realities? It would need a total disregard for man's powers of observation and honesty before one could throw out the complete body of firsthand witness accounts. We also have the footprints, hairs, faeces, and Roger Patterson's cine film, all soft evidence but nevertheless difficult to discard except by a total sceptic with a complete incapacity for new ideas. We believe that the evidence speaks for itself, in a voice too loud to be ignored for much longer.

NOTES

Where only author and book title are given, publication details can be found in the Bibliography. The book page references relate to the first edition listed in the Bibliography, unless otherwise noted.

1. Bigfoot in North America

1. Toronto, *Star*, 6 May 1982.
2. *Exeter Watchman*, 22 Sept 1818.
3. Mankato, MN, *Weekly Record*, 23 Jan 1869, reported in *Bigfoot Co-op*, June 1982, p.3.
4. Williamsport, PA, *Sun Gazette*, 30 Sept 1874.
5. Manchester, CT, *Journal Inquirer*, 24 Aug 1982.
6. In his paper 'Stoneclad Among the Cherokees' in Halpin and Ames, *Manlike Monsters on Trial*. This book contains 8 papers on manlike monsters in American Indian lore and art. See also Loren E. Coleman and Mark A. Hall, 'Some Bigfoot Traditions of the North American Tribes', *INFO Journal*, vol.2 (1970), pp.2-10.
7. This and other Indian Bigfoot lore is recorded in several books: Hugo Reid, *The Indians of Los Angeles County* (1926); Fray Geronimo Boscana, *Chinigchinich* (1933); Bernice E. Johnston, *California's Gabrielino Indians – Interviews by John Peabody Harrington* (1964). This material was located by Peter Guttilla, and noted in *Bigfoot Co-op*, Dec 1981, p.6.
8. Report in *Bigfoot Co-op*, Oct 1982, p.11.
9. Reports from West Palm Beach, FL, *Post*, 10 Oct 1980, and Covington, KY, *Post and Times Star*, 10 June 1982, reprinted in UFO Newsclipping Service (hereinafter UFONS), no.137 p.15 and no.157 p.18.

10. Newark, NJ, *Star Ledger*, 29 June 1981, reprinted in UFONS, no.144, p.19.
11. Details of Freeman case compiled from reports in *The Vancouver Sun*, 19, 22, 23 Oct 1982, and *The ISC Newsletter*, vol.1, no.2 (summer 1982), and vol.1, no.3 (autumn 1982).
12. Two Canadian reports from Green, *On the Track of the Sasquatch*, pp.192-4.
13. Isabel Davis and Ted Bloecher, *Close Encounter at Kelly and Others of 1955* (Evanston, IL: Center for UFO Studies, 1978) pp.162-5.
14. Brookings, SD, *Register*, 28 Sept 1979, reprinted in UFONS, Nov 1979, p.14.
15. For details see Bord, *The Bigfoot Casebook*, pp.17-18; the book records a number of more recent cases of Bigfeet less than 5 feet (1.5 metres) in height.
16. For a detailed report by Roe of this particularly good sighting, see Bord, *Alien Animals*, p.164, or *The Bigfoot Casebook*, p.58.
17. *INFO Journal*, no.26, p.15.
18. Pasadena, TX, *News-Citizen*, 16 May 1982, reprinted in UFONS, no.156, p.15.
19. Report from Rella Morris printed in *Bigfoot Co-op*, Aug 1981, pp.8-9.
20. Compiled from reports in a Greenville, SC, newspaper (title and precise date unknown) of Nov 1981, and the Port Huron, MI, *Times Herald*, 9 Dec 1981 and 29 Jan 1982, reprinted in UFONS, no.149, p.16; no.150, p.19; and no.152, p.18.
21. Full report quoted in Bord, *The Bigfoot Casebook*, pp.98-100.
22. Des Moines, IA, *Register*, 9 May 1980, noted in *Bigfoot Co-op*, June 1980, p.5.
23. Hunter with Dahinden, *Sasquatch*, pp.107-8; Green, *On the Track of the Sasquatch*, pp.81-2.
24. Napier, *Bigfoot*, p.169.
25. Hunter with Dahinden, op. cit., pp.141-3.
26. ibid., pp.199-202.
27. Clark and Coleman, *Creatures of the Outer Edge*, p.115.
28. Green, op. cit., p.163.
29. Green, *Sasquatch: The Apes Among Us*, p.444.
30. Sanderson, *Abominable Snowmen*, p.343.

2. Bigfoot in the Himalayas and USSR

1. *Among the Himalayas* (London, 1899), p.223; see also Sanderson, *Abominable Snowmen*, pp.1-3.
2. Edward W. Cronin, Jr., 'Recent Evidence of the Yeti, an Unknown Primate, from the Himalayas', *Pursuit*, vol.9, no.3, pp.63-5.
3. Dayton, Ohio, *Daily News*, 20 Mar 1975, and Pittsburgh, PA, *Press*, 13 Jan 1975.
4. London, UK, *Sunday Express*, 6 Feb 1977; *Climber and Rambler*, Apr 1977, p.11.
5. *Shropshire Star*, 31 May 1979; Simon Welfare and John Fairley, *Arthur C. Clarke's Mysterious World* (London: Collins, 1980), pp.15-16.
6. Heuvelmans, *On the Track of Unknown Animals*, p.94.
7. ibid., pp.114-16, which also details other native sightings.
8. Napier, *Bigfoot*, p.54.
9. Willy Ley, *Exotic Zoology* (Capricorn Books Edn, 1966), p.84.
10. On excreta and scalps, see Heuvelmans, op. cit., pp.117-21. For a list of sightings and tracks during 1887-1960 see Sanderson, *Abominable Snowmen*, pp.260-4.
11. Welfare and Fairley, op. cit., pp.18-19.
12. London: Weidenfeld and Nicolson, 1956.
13. Sanderson, op. cit., p.266.
14. Heuvelmans, op. cit., p.122.
15. Information on the three sizes of Yeti comes from ibid., p.123.
16. Napier, op. cit., p.150.
17. Heuvelmans, op. cit., pp.101-4.
18. Calcutta, India, *The Statesman*, 21 Jan 1982.
19. Heuvelmans, op. cit., pp.124-5.
20. *The Christian Science Monitor*, 18 Apr 1979.
21. Edward W. Cronin, Jr., 'Tracking the Yeti in the Snowfields of the Himalayas', *Pursuit*, vol.15, no.3, p.130.
22. Dr John Napier discusses the possible candidates – bears, birds, fakirs, langurs, orangutans – in *Bigfoot*, pp.143-61; and except for the Shipton footprint (he had not of course seen the Cronin footprint) would have dismissed the Yeti as a 'red herring' – p.205.
23. See Gordon Creighton's 'List of Names and Terms so far

Identified throughout the World as possibly Denoting Various Types of "Remnant Hominids"' (containing 131 names and still incomplete) in Tchernine, *The Yeti*, pp.173-81.

24. Sanderson, op. cit., pp.319-20.
25. ibid., p.320; Tchernine, op. cit., pp.59-60.
26. Details of Khakhlov's reports from Sanderson, op. cit., pp.313-18 and Tchernine, op. cit., pp.42-5.
27. Report from Dmitri Bayanov, printed in *Bigfoot Co-op*, June 1981, p.8.
28. *Hans Schiltberger's Journey into Heathen Parts*, c.AD 1430, ref. L1603.B1.210^v in the Manuscripts Department of the Municipal Library in Munich, mentioned by Myra Shackley in her paper 'The Case for Neanderthal Survival: Fact, Fiction or Faction?', *Antiquity*, LVI (1982), p.39.
29. For a detailed physical description see Shackley, *Wildmen*, pp.117-19.
30. Tchernine, op. cit., pp.47-8.
31. ibid., p.48.
32. ibid., pp.28-9.
33. *The Soviet Press – Current Digest*, 8 Sept 1979, pp.13-14.
34. Igor Bourtsev, 'Expedition "Gissar-80"', *Bigfoot Co-op*, June 1981, pp.9-11.
35. ibid., but taken from Bourtsev's full report, not the *Bigfoot Co-op* condensation.
36. Igor Bourtsev's preliminary report on the 1981 expedition in *Bigfoot Co-op*, Dec 1982, p.11.
37. For details of a 1970s interview with Karapetyan, and a more detailed account of his meeting with an Almas, see Henry Gris and William Dick, *The New Soviet Psychic Discoveries* (London: Souvenir Press, 1979), pp.183-9, 195-6.
38. ibid., p.192.
39. Sanderson, op. cit., pp.291-5.
40. Dr Kofman's research is reported in Gris and Dick, op. cit., pp.190-7.
41. The full story of Zana can be found in Tchernine, op. cit., pp.155-9.
42. Report from Dmitri Bayanov of the Darwin Museum, Moscow, in *Bigfoot Co-op*, Apr 1981, pp.10-11.

43. Tchernine, op. cit., pp.137-8.
44. 'What is it? . . . Myth or Reality?', *Technical Journal for Youth*, no.6.
45. ibid.
46. Sanderson, op. cit., pp.371-2.
47. Tchernine, op. cit., p.138.
48. In *Soviet Ethnography*; reprinted in English in Green, *On the Track of the Sasquatch*, pp.152-5, followed by John Green's comments.
49. Sanderson, op. cit., p.326.
50. Shackley, *Wildmen*.

3. Bigfoot in China, Australia, South-East Asia, Africa and South America

1. *The New York Times*, 5 Jan 1980, p.5.
2. Ji Ti, 'China has its Yeti Too', *International Wildlife*, Jan-Feb 1981, pp.18-19.
3. Canberra, Australia, *Times*, 8 Feb 1981.
4. Yuan Zhenxin and Huang Wanpo, *Wildman: China's Yeti*, pp.6-7. This 22-page booklet is 'Fortean Times' Occasional Paper No.1, published in 1981 and available from: BM – Fortean Times, London WC1N 3XX.
5. San Jose, CA, *Mercury*, 26 Feb 1981, reprinted in UFONS, no.141, p.16.
6. Fan Jingquan, 'I Witnessed a "Wildman" Mother and Child in the Chestnut Forest', in Yuan Zhenxin and Huang Wanpo, op. cit., pp.15-17.
7. Canberra, Australia, *Times*, 8 Feb 1981, reprinted in UFONS, no.142, p.16.
8. Ji Ti, op. cit., p.19.
9. ibid., p.19.
10. ibid., p.19.
11. Yuan Zhenxin and Huang Wanpo, op. cit., pp.9-10.
12. A fuller physical description is given in ibid., p.11.
13. ibid., pp.11-12.
14. Quoted in the Los Angeles, CA, *Times*, 28 Aug 1980, reprinted in UFONS, no.135, p.17.
15. A number of these reports have been collected together by Graham C. Joyner and published in booklet form in 1977 as 'The Hairy Man of South Eastern Australia'.

16. Diary account sent by Mrs Eileen Cox of Noosa Heads to *Australasian Post*, 28 Feb 1980, reprinted in UFONS, no.128, p.20.
17. Lismore, NSW, *The Northern Star*, 7 July 1977.
18. Don Boyd, 'Zowie! Where's the Yowie?', *Outdoors*, June 1978, pp.82-3.
19. ibid.
20. *Sun Herald*, 13 May 1977.
21. Boyd, op. cit.
22. Report from Australian newspaper, name unknown, 7 Apr 1978.
23. Sydney *Sunday*, 6 May 1979.
24. *Evening Post*, 18 Apr 1979.
25. *Australasian Post*, 28 Feb 1980, reprinted in UFONS, no.128, p.19.
26. Lismore, NSW, *The Northern Star*, 23 May 1981.
27. Boyd, op. cit.
28. Lismore, NSW, *The Northern Star*, 17 Aug 1977.
29. Details in *Bigfoot Co-op*, Feb 1981, pp.10-11.
30. *Pakistani Times*, 12 June 1969, quoted in *Pursuit*, vol.2, no.3, p.54.
31. *Pursuit*, vol.3, no.2, p.36.
32. AP report from Kuala Lumpur, 1 Aug 1971.
33. Sanderson, *Abominable Snowmen*, pp.229-30.
34. *Pursuit*, vol.3, no.2, p.36.
35. Heuvelmans, *On the Track of Unknown Animals*, p.79; Napier comments on 'reversed feet' in *Bigfoot*, pp.25-6.
36. Full report quoted in Sanderson, op. cit., pp.221-4, and Heuvelmans, op. cit., pp.85-6. Heuvelmans' Chapter 5 is devoted to the Orang Pendek, and Sanderson's Chapter 10 describes the man-beast situation throughout South-east Asia.
37. Napier, *Bigfoot*, p.26.
38. *News Extra*, 13 Oct 1974. See also Bord, *Alien Animals*, p.180.
39. Christchurch, NZ, *Truth*, 22 Dec 1982, reprinted in UFONS, no.163, p.19.
40. Katharine Scherman, *Spring on an Arctic Island* (London: Victor Gollancz, 1956), pp.156-64; see also Ivan T. Sanderson, *"Things"* (New York: Pyramid Books, 1967), pp.94-100.

41. In his chapter on Africa in *Abominable Snowmen*, ch.10.

42. *Discovery*, Dec 1937, reprinted in ibid., pp.190-1.

43. Report sent to *Discovery*, reprinted in ibid., p.191.

44. Heuvelmans, op. cit., ch. 16.

45. All material on 'X' from *Chicago Tribune*, 11 Oct 1978.

46. Sanderson, *Abominable Snowmen*, p.172; he describes the South American situation in pp.167-81.

47. Pablo Latapi Ortega, 'Ucumar, the Argentinian Yeti', *Contactos Extraterrestres* magazine, 16 Apr 1980.

48. Sanderson, *"Things"*, op. cit., pp.92-3.

49. Heuvelmans, op. cit., pp.204-5; Sanderson, *Abominable Snowmen*, p.174.

50. pp.80-93.

51. UPI report published in many US newspapers in late May 1976, e.g. St Louis, MO, *Post-Dispatch*, 23 May 1976.

52. Heuvelmans, op. cit., pp.203-4.

53. ibid., p.214; see also Sanderson, *Abominable Snowmen*, pp.178-81.

54. Pino Turolla, *Beyond the Andes* (New York: Harper and Row), pp.132-6.

55. Warren Smith, *Lost Cities of the Ancients – Unearthed!* (Zebra Books, 1976), pp.36-9.

56. Sanderson, *Abominable Snowmen*, pp.164-5.

57. The lore was reported in the University of Pennsylvania *Museum Journal*, vol.VI, no.3 (Sept 1915) and reprinted in Sanderson, *Abominable Snowmen*, pp.160-2.

4. Material Evidence and Behaviour Patterns

1. George Harrison, 'Modern Monsters', *Sports Afield*, Nov 1982. The author was Managing Editor of *National Wildlife*, and in 1970 was part of an expedition in the Mount St Helens area of Washington searching for Bigfoot. They found the tracks he described in his article, but did not see Bigfoot.

2. Napier, *Bigfoot*, pp.123-4.

3. See for example his two papers on Sasquatch foot anatomy in Sprague and Krantz, *The Scientist Looks at the Sasquatch*. Also good coverage of the footprint evidence can be found in John Green's books *On the Track of the Sasquatch* (ch.6) and *Sasquatch: The Apes Among Us* (ch.19).

4. Everett, WA, *Herald*, 27 May 1981, reprinted in UFONS, no.143, p.17. Dr John Napier also writes in detail on bear tracks in *Bigfoot*, pp.129-30, 150.

5. As reported by the witness in 1972 to Vladimir Pushkarev and quoted in his article 'New Evidence', *Technical Journal for Youth*, no.6 (1979), translation printed in *Bigfoot Co-op*, Feb 1983, p.8.

6. Interview with John Green by Peter Guttilla, in *Bigfoot Co-op*, Dec 1982, p.9.

7. Report by Linda Williford in *Bigfoot Co-op*, Aug 1982, pp.9-11.

8. An interesting account of the process of analysis is given in Vaughn M. Bryant, Jr., and Burleigh Trevor-Deutsch, 'Analysis of Feces and Hair Suspected to be of Sasquatch Origin', in Halpin and Ames, *Manlike Monsters on Trial*, pp.291-300.

9. Roe's full report is given in Bord, *The Bigfoot Casebook*, pp.58-60.

10. Wapakoneta, OH, *Daily News*, 18 March 1981, reprinted in UFONS, no.143, p.15.

11. Yuan Zhenxin and Huang Wanpo, *Wild Man*, Fortean Times Occasional Paper No.1, p.10.

12. The problems are highlighted by John Green in *Sasquatch: The Apes Among Us*, pp.284-6.

13. Sanderson, *Abominable Snowmen*, p.335.

14. Yuan Zhenxin and Huang Wanpo, op. cit., p.9.

15. Dr Heuvelmans tells the full story in his *L'Homme de Néanderthal est Toujours Vivant*, and Dr Napier gives a shorter version in *Bigfoot*, pp.98-114.

16. There is as yet no book devoted solely to the Patterson film, though one is in preparation. A clear account of the events and their aftermath is given in Green, *Sasquatch: The Apes Among Us*, ch.6. More information and analysis can be found in Ivan T. Sanderson, *More "Things"* (New York: Pyramid Books, 1969), pp.65-79; Napier, *Bigfoot*, pp.89-95; Green, *On the Track of the Sasquatch*, pp.70-4; Hunter with Dahinden, *Sasquatch*, pp.116-28, 180-6; and five colour enlargements from the film are reproduced in Halpin and Ames, *Manlike Monsters on Trial*.

17. Green, *Sasquatch: The Apes Among Us*, p.129.

18. Jon Beckjord, 'Comments on the Patterson/Gimlin film', *Bigfoot Co-op*, June 1981, p.5.

19. Bruce Bonney, 'Comments on Jon Beckjord's "Baby"', *Bigfoot Co-op*, Dec 1981, pp.9-11.

20. Berwick, PA, *Press-Enterprise*, 26 Aug 1980, reprinted in UFONS, no.135, p.19.

21. David Hadaller, 'Sasquatch: The Nature of the Beast', *The Oregonian Northwest Magazine*, 24 Oct 1982, reprinted in UFONS, no.161, p.17.

22. For more details and photographs see Bord, *The Bigfoot Casebook*, pp.139-41.

23. Berwick, PA, *Press-Enterprise*, 26 Aug 1980, reprinted in UFONS, no.135, p.19.

24. ibid.

25. Peter Jenkins, *A Walk Across America*, noted in *Bigfoot Co-op*, Apr 1981, p.7.

26. The full story of how the recordings were obtained is given in Slate and Berry, *Bigfoot*, chs. 1, 2, 3; the analysis is described in R. Lynn Kirlin and Lasse Hertel, 'Estimates of Pitch and Vocal Tract Length from Recorded Vocalizations of Purported Bigfoot', in Halpin and Ames, op. cit., pp.274-90.

27. Green, *Sasquatch: The Apes Among Us*, p.442.

28. Carlsbad, NM, *Current-Argus*, 28 Oct 1980, reprinted in UFONS, no.138, p.20.

29. Reported by John Fuhrmann/Peter Guttilla to *Bigfoot Co-op*, Dec 1981, p.3.

30. *Idaho State Journal*, 11 Sept 1980, noted in *Bigfoot Co-op*, Dec 1980, p.8.

31. San Diego, CA, *Union*, 17 Aug 1982, noted in *Bigfoot Co-op*, Oct 1982, p.5.

32. Reported by John Green to *Bigfoot Co-op*, Feb 1981, p.2.

33. Green, *Sasquatch: The Apes Among Us*, p.378.

34. The Barone incident is reported in more detail in ch.1; the Hensley report is from Port Huron, MI, *Times Herald*, 15 Dec 1981, reprinted in UFONS, no.151, p.18.

35. Lancaster, CA, *Ledger-Gazette*, 27 Aug 1980, noted in *Bigfoot Co-op*, Oct 1980, p.4.

36. Carlsbad, NM, *Current-Argus*, 2 Nov 1980, reprinted in UFONS, no.140, p.17.

37. Green, *Sasquatch: The Apes Among Us*, p.425.
38. San Jose, CA, *Mercury News*, 1 Jan 1981, noted in *Bigfoot Co-op*, June 1981, p.4.
39. Aberdeen, WA, *Daily World*, 22 Apr 1982, reprinted in UFONS, no.155, p.17.
40. Green, *Sasquatch: The Apes Among Us*, pp.421-5.
41. CA, *Trinity Journal*, 16 Feb 1961.
42. Vancouver, WA, *The Columbian*, 7 and 9 May 1979, noted in *Bigfoot Co-op*, Feb 1981, p.5.
43. Green, *Sasquatch: The Apes Among Us*, p.57.
44. ibid., p.269.

5. Non-Physical Bigfoot and the UFO Link

1. West Palm Beach, FL, *Post*, 10 Oct 1980, reprinted in UFONS, no.137, p.15.
2. Bord, *The Bigfoot Casebook*, p.129.
3. ibid., p.139.
4. Shelby, NC, *Daily Star*, 16 Sept 1981, reprinted in UFONS, no.148, p.18.
5. Clark and Coleman, *Creatures of the Outer Edge*, p.81.
6. Report by the grandson of the witness, Bruce G. Hallenbeck, in Chatham, NY, *Courier*, 9 April 1981.
7. Slate and Berry, *Bigfoot*, pp.118-20.
8. Clark and Coleman, op. cit., p.81.
9. Stan Gordon, 'UFO-Related Bigfoot Encounter in Pennsylvania', *The MUFON UFO Journal*, no.171 pp.3-5. Gordon gave pseudonyms for the witnesses, but as their real names were used in press reports there seems no point in concealing their true identity. For a sample press report see Johnstown, PA, *Tribune-Democrat*, 7 Nov 1981, reprinted in UFONS, no.151, p.17.
10. Stan Gordon, 'UFO-Bigfoot Update', *The MUFON UFO Journal*, no.173, p.13.
11. Australian Centre for UFO Studies, 1980.
12. Keel, *Strange Creatures from Time and Space*, p.116.
13. Dr Berthold Eric Schwarz, 'UFOs; Delusion or Dilemma?', *Flying Saucer Review* Special Issue No.2, 'Beyond Condon' (1969) pp.49-51.
14. Stan Gordon, 'UFOs, in Relation to Creature Sightings in Pennsylvania', *MUFON UFO Symposium Proceedings 1974*, p.142.

15. Clark and Coleman, op. cit., pp.82-3.
16. Reported by Len Stringfield in *Skylook*, and noted in *Canadian UFO Report*, vol.3, no.4, pp.5-6.
17. Jerome Clark, 'The Frightened Creature on County Road W', *Flying Saucer Review*, vol.21, no.1, pp.20-1.
18. A very full report, with a psychiatric analysis of the chief witness, is given by Dr Berthold Eric Schwarz in his paper 'Berserk: A UFO-Creature Encounter', *Flying Saucer Review*, vol.20, no.1, pp.3-11.
19. Reported in the Santiago paper *La Segunda*, and later in *La Razón* of Buenos Aires, Argentina, 18 Nov 1979; translation in UFONS, no.126, p.16.
20. A full report has been compiled by investigator Dennis Pilichis, *Night Siege: The Northern Ohio UFO Creature Invasion*, privately published from PO Box 5012, Rome, Ohio 44085.
21. Jerome Clark and Loren Coleman, 'Anthropoids, Monsters and UFOs', *Flying Saucer Review*, vol.19, no.1, p.18.
22. Sebastion Robiou Lamarche, 'UFOs and Mysterious Deaths of Animals', *Flying Saucer Review*, vol.22, no.6, pp.7-8.
23. Letter to the authors from Dr P. M. H. Edwards, 20 Sept 1982, to whom Mrs Cross had told her story.
24. Research by Peter Guttilla recorded in *Bigfoot Co-op*, Dec 1981, p.6.
25. Said to be from a journal written by the grandfather of James C. Wyatt of Memphis, Tennessee, and sent to author Brad Steiger who published the report in his *Mysteries of Time and Space* (London: Sphere Books, 1977), pp.117-19.
26. Stan Gordon, 'UFO-Related Bigfoot Encounter in Pennsylvania', *The MUFON UFO Journal*, no.171, p.3.

6. Searching for Answers

1. Portland, OR, *Oregonian*, 13 Apr 1982, reprinted in UFONS, no.154, p.18; see also Los Angeles, CA, *Times*, 4 June 1982, reprinted in UFONS, no.157, pp.15-16.
2. Clarendon, AR, *Arkansas Democrat*, 26 Oct 1982, noted in *Bigfoot Co-op*, Feb 1983, p.2.
3. Vancouver, WA, *Columbian*, 3 and 6 Dec 1982, noted in *Bigfoot Co-op*, Feb 1983, p.3.
4. They eventually wrote to Roger Patterson, presumably

having by then heard of Bigfoot through the publicity he was obtaining, and the report is noted in John Green's *The Sasquatch File*, p.39.

5. Buckley, WA, *News Banner*, 19 Oct 1972, noted in *Bigfoot Co-op*, June 1980, p.2.

6. Port Huron, MI, *Times Herald*, 28 Nov 1981, reprinted in UFONS, no.151, p.17.

7. Portland, OR, *Oregonian*, 24 Oct 1982, reprinted in UFONS, no.161, pp.17-18.

8. Schenectady, NY, *Gazette*, 11 May 1981, reprinted in UFONS, no.142, p.18.

9. San Francisco, CA, *Examiner and Chronicle*, 11 July 1982, reprinted in UFONS, no.158, p.14.

10. Dmitri Bayanov, 'Why it is Not Right to Kill a Gentle Giant', *Pursuit*, vol.13, no.4, pp.140-1.

11. See Heuvelmans, *L'Homme de Néanderthal est Toujours Vivant*.

12. Sanderson, *Abominable Snowmen*, pp.355-74.

13. ibid., p.374.

14. p.111.

15. David Hadaller, 'Sasquatch, The Nature of the Beast', in Portland, OR, *Oregonian*, 24 Oct 1982, reprinted in UFONS, no.161, pp.17-18.

16. Sanderson, op. cit., p.370.

17. Yuan Zhenxin and Huang Wanpo, 'A Challenge to Science', in Yuan Zhenxin and Huang Wanpo, *Wild Man*, Fortean Times Occasional Paper No.1, p.14.

18. In his chapter on fossil evidence in *Bigfoot*, pp.173-92.

19. Napier, op. cit., p.183.

20. Sanderson, op. cit., pp.417-19.

21. Di Francis, *Cat Country: The Quest for the British Big Cat* (Newton Abbot: David and Charles, 1983).

22. In a letter to the authors, dated 30 Dec 1982.

23. An earlier attempt to explain the link between mystery animals and UFOs, and to identify the possible energy sources involved, can be read in Chapter 6 of our *Alien Animals*.

24. R. Martin Wolf, 'Coherence in Chaos', *Pursuit*, vol.11, no.1, p.34.

25. See for example Paul Devereux, *Earth Lights* (Wellingborough: Turnstone Press, 1982).

26. Dr Michael A. Persinger, 'Predicting UFO Events and Experiences', *Thirteenth Annual MUFON UFO Symposium Proceedings*, 1982, pp.34-9.
27. John A. Keel, 'The "Superior" Technology', *Flying Saucer Review*, vol.15, no.5, pp.26-7.
28. Report by Peter Guttilla in *Bigfoot Co-op*, Feb 1981, p.6.
29. Letter to the authors dated 7 Sept 1982.
30. Devereux, op. cit.
31. D. Scott Rogo, *The Haunted Universe* (New York: Signet Book, New American Library, 1977), p.150.
32. John Michell & Robert J. M. Rickard, *Living Wonders* (London: Thames and Hudson, 1982), p.44.

BIBLIOGRAPHY

Bord, Janet & Colin, *Alien Animals*, London: Paul Elek, 1980; Harrisburg, PA: Stackpole Books, 1981.
—*The Bigfoot Casebook*, London: Granada Publishing, 1982; Harrisburg, PA: Stackpole Books, 1982.
Clark, Jerome, and Loren Coleman, *Creatures of the Outer Edge*, New York: Warner Books, 1978.
Green, John, *The Sasquatch File*, Victoria, BC: Cheam Publishing (1299 Tracksell Avenue, Victoria, BC, V8P 2C8, Canada), 1973.
—*On the Track of the Sasquatch* (incorporating *On the Track of the Sasquatch* and *Year of the Sasquatch*), New York: Ballantine Books, 1973; published individually by Cheam Publishing, BC, 1968, 1970, and revised editions published 1980 as *On the Track of the Sasquatch*, Books I and II.
—*Sasquatch: The Apes Among Us*, Victoria, BC: Cheam Publishing, 1978; Seattle, Hancock House Publishers, 1978.
Halpin, Marjorie M., and Michael M. Ames (eds), *Manlike Monsters on Trial: Early Records and Modern Evidence*, Vancouver, BC: University of British Columbia Press, 1980 (contains a useful 18-page 'Bibliography: Published Materials Concerning the Abominable Snowman, the Yeti, the Sasquatch, and Related Hominidae' by L. G. M. Ruus).
Heuvelmans, Dr Bernard, *On the Track of Unknown Animals*, New York: Hill and Wang Inc., 1965; London: Paladin Books, 1970.
—*L'Homme de Néanderthal est Toujours Vivant* (co-author Dr Boris Porchnev), Paris: Plon, 1974.
—*Les Bêtes Humaines d'Afrique*, Paris: Plon, 1980.

Hunter, Don, with René Dahinden, *Sasquatch*, Toronto, Ont.: McClelland & Stewart, 1973; Scarborough, Ont.: New American Library of Canada, 1975.

Izzard, Ralph W. B., *The Abominable Snowman Adventure*, London: Hodder & Stoughton, 1955; Garden City, NY: Doubleday (title *The Abominable Snowman*).

Keel, John A., *Strange Creatures from Time and Space*, Greenwich, CT: Fawcett Publications, 1970; London, Neville Spearman, 1975; London: Sphere Books, 1976.

Napier, Dr John, *Bigfoot: The Yeti and Sasquatch in Myth and Reality*, London: Jonathan Cape, 1972; London: Abacus Books, 1976; New York: Dutton, 1973.

Patterson, Roger, *Do Abominable Snowmen of America Really Exist?*, Yakima, WA: Franklin Press, 1966.

Sanderson, Ivan T., *Abominable Snowmen: Legend Come to Life*, Philadelphia: Chilton Book Co., 1961; New York: Jove Publications, revised abridgement, 1977.

Shackley, Dr Myra, *Wildmen: Yeti, Sasquatch and the Neanderthal Enigma*, London: Thames and Hudson, 1983; New York: Thames and Hudson, 1983 (title *Still Living?*).

Slate, B. Ann, and Alan Berry, *Bigfoot*, New York: Bantam Books, 1976.

Sprague, Roderick, and Grover S. Krantz (eds), *The Scientist Looks at the Sasquatch*, Moscow, ID: The University Press of Idaho, 1977 (new edition with 3 new articles published 1979).

Stonor, Charles Robert, *The Sherpa and the Snowman*, London: Hollis and Carter, 1955.

Tchernine, Odette, *The Snowman and Company*, London: Robert Hale, 1961.

—*The Yeti*, London: Neville Spearman, 1970.

Wylie, Kenneth, *Bigfoot: A Personal Inquiry into a Phenomenon*, New York: Viking Penguin, 1980.

INDEX